FROM THE VALLEYS TO THE MOUNTAINS

...and overcoming some hills on the way

FROM THE VALLEYS TO THE MOUNTAINS

...and overcoming some hills on the way

The autobiography of

Terry Hanford

New Life Publishing Co.

Nottingham, England

First published in the UK in 2006

ISBN 9780-9536100-9-8

Printed by Creative Print and Design Group, Middlesex, England.

Contents

This book is dedicated to my dear wife, Sylvia, without whose commitment and unselfishness it would not have been possible, nor would my travelling around the world. She sacrificed so much to bless the missions. I include my daughter, Sharon, and son, Jason, who make up our small family and of whom I am proud.

Also my dear friend Peter Yates who has encouraged me and stood with me right through, and without whose sponsorship we could not have published.

I would also like to thank my patient and competent friend Cyril Cartwright for the countless days spent typing, setting up and preparing the manuscript for the printers, together with Mark, Jo and Adele who helped me get started, and Enid, Jean and Dave who proofread for me.

Acknowledgements also go to:
Laurence Hennesey, Breakfree Ministries. Tel: 01204 528108
Barry Woodward, evangelist. Tel: 01706 638803
Mary and Dave Andrews, Audio Productions.
Tel: 01204 431078

Foreword

Terry Hanford is a well-respected church leader in Assemblies of God in Great Britain. Through his wide experience of Christian ministry, Terry has shown himself to be creative, innovative, and an excellent communicator of the Gospel, both as a preacher and as a radio presenter and speaker.

My first working relationship with Terry goes back to the '70s, to a time when we worked together on youth camps. I quickly became aware of his passion for Christ, pastoral heart and communication skills of this man from Wales.

Throughout the years Terry has confirmed his calling in the churches he has pastored in Peterborough, Bristol, Exeter and Denton and through his activity in evangelism and radio work. It has been said that the true stature of a leader is demonstrated in how they handle good times, hard times and ordinary times. Terry has shone in all three. I have been challenged as I have watched him maintain his faith, dignity, love of God and people through severe personal illness.

The mosaic of a person's life is shaped through their experience in life. I have enjoyed the story of Terry's life through this autobiography and know that it will bring inspiration, humour and encouragement to all who want to live a fulfilled life that is pleasing to God.

Paul C Weaver
General Superintendent
Assemblies of God in Great Britain

"Pentecost"
Edited and Published by Donald Gee

A Review of World-wide Pentecostal Activity. Published at the Request of the Pentecostal World Conference

All subscriptions to "Pentecost," 36 & 37, Clapham Crescent, London, S.W.4, England

Editorial Address:—
49b PELHAM ROAD
LINDFIELD
HAYWARDS HEATH
SUSSEX, ENGLAND

August 31, 1965.

Pastor T.R.Hanford

It gives me great pleasure to commend Terence R. Hanford as a Pentecostal minister in good standing with Assemblies of God in Great Britain& Ireland.

He has a very acceptable ministry, and pastors a growing church in Bristol.

I had an exceptional opportunity to get to know him personally, as he was s Student in the Kenley Bible College during the period when I was the Principal. I formed a high opinion of his Christian character, and his suitability for the high calling of a minister of the Gospel of our Lord Jesus Christ. I believe he will prove a blessing to the people wherever he goes.

Donald Gee

Donald Gee,
Editor of PENTECOST.

Introduction

The sun was shining, the bells were ringing, and my father was pacing outside the bedroom of 35 Gladstone Street, in the small inconspicuous coal mining village called Aberaman, in one of the major valleys of South Wales, UK. At precisely 11am, when people were going to church, Colin was born. Before you get confused, yes, originally Colin, but quickly changed to Terry. For what reason I do not know, maybe Terence Raymond Hanford sounded better in its full glory. I had no brothers or sisters, and in my early years felt very useless and untalented among my peers, except for one distinct assurance. I was being brought up to know and love the Lord Jesus. Soon my parents moved to join my godly grandparents in a large house named Belmont. This did mean that my uncle Alwyn became a big brother and my aunt Eunice a big sister to me. We were always a close family and have remained so ever since.

However it is time to do what they call today 'coming clean'. Why am I really writing this book? Michael J Fox the famous actor did it after seven years; David Jones, who turned the battered and almost bankrupt national retail group 'NEXT' into a multi-billion-pound success story, kept it secret from 1982 when he was 39 years of age. World boxing champion Mohammed Ali has faced it, and so has octogenarian Billy Graham, the world-famous evangelist, and so have tens of thousands of ordinary people like me. The day comes when the doctor sits you down and says, "Yes, you have Parkinson's disease," after 15 years of tests, scans and consultancies in London and Manchester; it was not Essential Tremor, but the real thing. PD is a degenerative neurological condition that is medically incurable but, like the high profile people I have referred to, I have not yet sat down and dropped out of life. I too, believing in a Sovereign God, want to tell my story to inspire and encourage those who may be facing almost insurmountable mountains today and also those who care for us. With God all things are possible – yes, even our healing. Until then we are going to climb. You would be amazed at the number of people who have contacted me when I said that three nervous breakdowns put me into hospital, with the accompanying stigma. So I pray that, again, 'coming clean' regarding PD will bring hope and help to many more ordinary folk like me. I am told that the servants of God should not divulge such personal things: it's being negative. I had to discern which voice to obey. Despite what the disease is doing to my body, I am enjoying – and sometimes enduring – the challenging route God has allowed me to take.

I now take a massive jump ahead to a time when I was praying in a Butlin's holiday chalet, just before going into the packed Prince's Ballroom with around 3,000 in attendance. Paul Yonggi Cho, pastor of the largest Pentecostal church in the world, from Seoul in South Korea, was the speaker and I was the chairman. My stomach was already turning over. Instructions sent to all chairmen had to be obeyed, including the positive discouraging of applause when people were introduced before ministry. Imagine my embarrassment when someone jumped up from behind me and said, "We should make an exception; in this case applause is in order." Standing before that huge crowd looking at me for direction, for this was the highlight of the week (there were probably 8,000 people present at the conference that year) I wished the floor would open and I could drop through.

Then, too, I well remember the dust-filled air in my home village, with its deadly diseases such as silicosis and various lung complaints, which contributed to the death of my grandad at 56, and of my father eventually at 85. I was deep in thought, enjoying the clean air in the Swiss Alps, high up in the mountains at Emmetten where I was giving seminars. on media subjects for the British Assemblies of God Broadcasting Council, e.g. presenting and producing programmes, interviewing and being interviewed etc. The untrained, frightened boy taught only by the Holy Spirit, and his own determination to learn from the godly examples and writings of master broadcasters. In fact I was part of the Revivaltime Quartet, who sang on the first Revivaltime programme from the British Assemblies of God over Radio Luxemburg. I looked with awe and admiration at the preacher, J N Parr, reaching lost souls with the Gospel burning in his heart... and mine. Silently I prayed, 'God, one day, give me a chance like that.' Naturally there was no hope, but then a letter came from the British Broadcasting Council, BBC Radio 2, that changed everything.

A mountain to climb, but then that's the story of my life, From the Valleys to the Mountains and how to overcome some hills on the way.

Please read:
1 Corinthians 1:27, 28
Judges 6:12-15
Exodus 4:10-12

For your loveliness and kindness you show,
For your wisdom and the way you, somehow,
seem to 'know',
Through many years of walking this glorious road,
But more than that...
You've been in the Master's presence
While He showed you His truth and His ways,
You've been down some difficult paths,
Seen uncertain dark days,
Till here you both stand,
Trophies of grace, held aloft in the palm of His hand,
For the likes of me to be blessed by who you are,
And to thank my God for the treasures
He's put in my heart so far, through you,
My spirit sings inside for I know He just loves
you both too.
I said, "Father... I love and appreciate them so much,
I need You to take my inadequate words
And anoint them with Your special touch,
So they don't just hear my heart,
But hear You say,
A supernatural 'Thank you',
Through my old familiar way."

By Joan Nichols

CHAPTER ONE

In the beginning

The valleys and mountains of Wales are very beautiful and, now that the coal mines have just about all been closed and landscaped over, the valleys look more beautiful than before. But in my early days as a normal average lad they played a very significant part in my life. You see we lived on the side of the mountain, where actually my mother still lives, not a big mountain, but quite a gradient from the valley. It was an incline up the hill to our house. But across the valley, probably about a mile away, there is another mountain. And on that mountainside my best friend Alan Williams lived in a farmhouse. It was possible for us by means of using different coloured flags to convey messages to each other from one side of the valley to the other. This saved a lot of walking and we were able by this strange means to convey to each other messages: where we'd meet at a certain time, or where we would be going, and so the valleys and mountains played a very significant part in my life at that time. We did find that when mountain climbing, when we thought we'd got to the top of the mountain, there was yet another mountain to climb which was often the case. Mountains played a big part in the life of Jesus too.

Mountains have a great significance in the Bible:

- Mount Moriah where Abraham was prepared to sacrifice Isaac;
- Mount Horeb where Moses saw the burning bush;

- Mount Sinai where Moses received the Law;
- Mount Carmel where fire fell and Elijah defeated Baal;
- Mount Hermon where Christ was transfigured;
- Mount Calvary where Christ was crucified;
- Mount of Olives where Christ ascended to heaven and will return.

Mountains have a great significance in my life. I was born on the side of one, did some preaching practice on one like my grandad, received a vision of the lost on one and a burden for Denton from Werneth Low Country Park in north-west England, and received the key to open radio waves to Bolton as I looked over Greater Manchester from the Pennines.

I learned as a boy to fix my eyes on the summit if I wanted to get to the top. I learned you would get there one step at a time. On the way up your legs felt like jelly until you got your second wind, then it was as easy to walk on the top, as it was to walk along the bottom. The view is better, the air is clearer, the noise has gone, it seems God is nearer. I learned to appreciate the mountains and, just like Moses, you get your plans on the mountain far easier than in the valley. Never make a big decision when in the valley of depression. Keep climbing because the devil never gets tired. Get your word from God and hold on to it and don't let go. I see today a great stealing going on by the devil. The people of God must hold on to their rights in Christ.

Certainly in the New Testament, but in the Old Testament too, we have the very significant happenings of Moses going up into the mountains to find the pattern and plan for the future of the children of Israel. And they seemed to befriend me and I did very well. In hospital I was well looked after and I came out well. They were difficult times during the war with so much rationing, and I well remember when bananas first came over into our country and into some of the shops in Aberdare, the town near where I lived, my mother queuing for hours just to buy a couple of bananas. There were times of course when air-raid shelters were necessary to protect us, when the alarms and the hooters went off, giving us notice that there was a flight of enemy planes coming over, though more often than not we would hide under the stairs. They were frightening days, but we were well cared for and God preserved us. We were living at the time in Belmont, with my gran and grandfather. My grandad died at 56, with Parkinson's disease. They say today that you can't die from it, but from associated things, and of course he did have silicosis and some of the lung diseases associated with his work down in the coal mines. But I remember him shaking very violently, so much so that there were times when my grandmother had to bind him up in the chair because he would just flop on the floor and hurt himself. It was a very dark day, very terrible day, even in the life of a little boy, when Grandad whom I loved, went to be with Jesus. He was a great preacher, and he was treasurer of our local Pentecostal church for more years than I can remember. In fact his son, my Uncle Alwyn, took on the position after him, and remained treasurer up until very recent times. Grandad used to preach to the sheep and the cattle on the mountains. That's where he served his apprenticeship. My grandma did have a very humorous side to her and there were times when, unbeknown to him, when he was up in the Graig mountain, she would hide behind a tree and suddenly jump out when Grandad was in full flow and say, "You silly fool! What on earth are you doing, who are you preaching to?" And then of course they'd come down the mountain hand in hand. I had a godly grandma and grandad, and really grandma brought me up almost as much as my mother because we lived in the same house, and I loved them very dearly. Grandma used to look after the preachers. Almost all the preachers who came to the Aberaman Pentecostal church stayed with my gran, she was a great host and a great cook.

The Christian influence of my mother's side of the family won me over, although I loved sport and won some trophies for athletics and cricket. The tradition of preachers in the family was highlighted in my grandmother's home by a very large, ornate, gilded, illuminated address hung in the dining room. The text is in Welsh (the translation is below) and was presented to my grandmother's grandfather. He resigned during the initial year of the Welsh Revival – 1904, when many were filled with the Holy Spirit and spoke in 'tongues' and were put out of the churches. So 'cottage meetings' started and continued until 1924 when Assemblies of God was founded. My grandfather was a leader in the early days of these events in the Welsh valleys. At the conference of the East Glamorgan Assembly held at Hebron, Dowlais on the 22nd June 1903 presided over by the Rev D C Jones, Penygraig, it was proposed by Alderman Edward Thomas (Cocharf-Redbeard) J P, seconded by Evan Owen Esq JP, and unanimously resolved that the delegates of this conference accept with deep regret the resignation of the Rev Thomas Davies of Aberaman, the revered and industrious secretary of the Assembly. The translation is as follows:

> *The delegates wish to declare their sincere thanks to the Great Giver of All Goodness for the strength and abundant life given to our brother to fulfil the requirements of his important task over a long period of 21 years, with such exactness, correctness and success, for the deep and thorough interest which he revealed in his work and service for the Master and the wise and prudent and careful guidance which he gave to his brothers when dealing with the spiritual and other work pertaining to the chapels. They hope that Mr Davies will gain comfort and pleasure from the fact that the work of the Assembly has increased greatly since his election to the post in the year 1883. During these years membership through baptism increased by thousands, tens of thousands of chapels were built as Temples of the Most High, and hundreds of thousands of pounds were subscribed to expand the Kingdom of God: "this cometh from the Lord and is wonderful in our sight." They hope that this knowledge will cheer, gladden and support the thoughts and feeling of our beloved brother.*
>
> *With great feeling of admiration they wish to*

present this faithful brother to their Saviour in whose service he toiled so zealously and actively for so many years. While they hope that the eventide of his refined and worthy life will be light and clear and that he will have many more days to labour in his Saviour's vineyard, possessing the same zeal and activity which was characteristic of him in the past. They desire for him at the end of a full and successful career a full admission to the joy of the Lord.

Signed on behalf of the conference:

D C Jones	*Past President*
Edward Thomas	*President*
R E Williams	*Vice-President*
W G Howell	*Treasurer*
Evan Owen	*Treasurer*
W R Jones	*Secretary*
I Mills	*Assistant Secretary*

It did mean of course that I came to know and meet some of the great preachers of that era – Leonard Ravenhill, John Carter, Howard Carter and Donald Gee. Yes, Donald Gee, because we did have a bathroom. Not many had bathrooms at that time and Donald Gee used to like a six o'clock, cold bath every morning. Many of the worldwide preachers from different parts used to stay in Belmont. I was quite young, but I would remember them. We had reason to remember John Carter's visit because Sharon, who was a young child, loved to cuddle up to him and often went to sleep in his arms when he was having '40 winks' after Sunday dinner. It was embarrassing though when we entertained a rich American in our humble home. Sharon reminded him courteously to watch he didn't drop bits on Mummy's best carpet! Somewhere our pre-visitor little behaviour talk went wrong. I do remember a particular occasion with Leonard Ravenhill. He was leader of the Holiness church at the time and in later life went to work with David Wilkerson in New York. He used to preach in the open air, right opposite a public house, and he would invariably get the men who came out of the public house irate, because of his hellfire preaching, and his preaching against the evils of drink etc. I would be hiding behind my mother in a nearby shop entrance. And right in front of Leonard Ravenhill would stand my Aunt Eunice, as a kind of protection, because these men would quite easily – and indeed they would try to – come up and manhandle Leonard Ravenhill. But with a woman in front, she protected him. Great days, great men of God, great preachers, wonderful packed churches, wonderful conventions, great meetings. There, of course, young people met young people and oftentimes lifelong partnerships started, which happened to me in Gwawr Chapel, that was hired for a big youth rally, where I met my wife, Sylvia. The church was full, but these two lovely girls made room for Cyril my friend and me; they pushed up a bit, and from that close encounter began another life story which will unfold as we go through the book. We were brought up to love the Lord. Sunday school and youth meetings we loved, and later I became a Sunday school teacher. These were times when the Word of God was so powerful that even as children we were swept under the anointing of God's Spirit.

I remember when I was baptised in water and baptised in the Holy Spirit, when we had to link arms together as we walked home from church to our homes because we were so drunk in the Holy Spirit. The power of God was upon us. There was no doubt that probably from as early as I can remember I was a Christian. I loved the Lord, but the key distinct moments of conviction and conversion happened in a prayer meeting on the third Wednesday in October 1949, when I took Jesus Christ into my heart and life, and knew that something had happened within me. But even before then I knew God's blessing on my life. The call of God came at the age of 16. But I'm jumping ahead. We had great days of fun. I loved sport and was part of the church's 'unofficial' cricket team. In fact my dad who was not a Christian until later on in life used to join us. There were times when we played cricket in the street and smashed windows, then we would try to hide. Invariably we would be caught, pocket money being confiscated to pay for the damages. My best friend was Aeron Morgan, who is my cousin and at the present time lives in Australia. He now travels the world preaching and teaching and, in my estimation, is one of the finest Bible expositors of our generation. He and his fine wife, Dinah, remain close friends with us. He was the first General Superintendent of Assemblies of God in Britain and later went to Australia to be Principal of the Bible College. Aeron and I were and are great pals and we took every opportunity to play cricket or football in the appropriate season.

I went to the grammar school in Aberdare, took my O levels and was fairly successful, but then came the great decision. Was I going on to take my A levels and enter college or university? My dad wanted me to train to enter a profession. He would have liked me to be a doctor or a teacher but the call of God came at 16. I had a tremendous personal encounter with the Lord. I saw a vision of a church, a large church that was closed with people knocking at the doors wanting to get into the church, which to me signified people wanting to find hope in Christ, but there was no one to open the door. And so that little vision and various other events caused the call of God to intensify. But I had to go to work in between times, because I wanted to go to Kenley Bible College in Surrey, but I was repeatedly told I was far too young. I kept asking, begging, pleading, but I had to wait until I was around 21 years of age. That was two or three years ahead. So I worked in Aberdare Cables, in an office in the production department, for the princely wage of two pounds and ten pence a week – that's old money. That first wage packet my mother has kept all through the years. I wonder if the two pound notes are still in there for they could well be valuable. Unbeknown to me, my mother kept my wage unopened and gave me pocket money, but saved that money so that when I went into Bible college I had savings to cover the fees. My father took other jobs, apart from working down in the coal mines. He was excellent at practical things in the building line, particularly in masonry, and he did this to keep me in Bible college although he was not a Christian. I remember when I told him I was going to be baptised in water I saw the blood drain from his face. I think he was somewhat dismayed and upset but he knew that I had started on my life's journey then. God had a plan for my life, which I was determined to follow, but my dad always supported me – the most wonderful father that one could ever have, but very difficult to talk to about salvation until later on, which again is part of the story.

Whilst working at Aberdare Cables I was invited into the cricket team, for I enjoyed cricket and I was quite successful at it. I still have got in my filing cabinet the cricket ball that was presented to me when, in winning a match, I took six wickets for 14 runs. That was quite a highlight. For some time I kept the ball near the side of my bed in case anyone should invade our home. I don't know if I would be as accurate as David with his sling, but we have a bit of a laugh about it. My dad was so kind – when he came home obviously tired I would be waiting for him during the winter when the snow was on the ground, and I'd made a pile of snowballs for him just inside the back gate and some for me and we would have a snowball fight. Great fun. Dad built a wonderful concrete garage for me because they had bought a brand new car that I could sit in and only the best was good enough. At this time Dad, because we had a large shed at the top of the garden, used to keep chickens and kill them at Christmas for our Christmas meal. Thankfully I saw it on only one occasion, but it was so grotesque to me because he chopped the head off and I saw the chicken running around without a head: a headless chicken. I felt over the years that some Christians and indeed some churches have been like headless chickens, running around, but soon they flop. In fact if we're not connected with the Head who is Christ how can we ever find direction? We need to have a plan and blueprint from the mountain as Moses had it and to stop running around like headless chickens. We need to know where we're going and where we're leading the people. There were times too in that garden when my friendship with Aeron Morgan deepened. I shall never forget my mum and my grandmother putting food out for our dinner in the back garden, which was a big garden with a large lawn. Many times, being just boys, we would tip the table and the dinner would go all over the lawn; apart from making the lawn look a mess we had lost our dinner. They were the memories of the early days. The valleys and the mountains are so significant to us.

I learned to appreciate the teachings I had in the early days in my home assembly. I only really had one pastor until recent years and he was pastor Danny Davies. A great man of God, not an outstanding preacher, but a man who worked down in the colliery. He contracted silicosis, and one didn't have to turn round to tell when he was coming into the church, you heard him by the gasping of his breath. A man who walked with God, someone who could stand up when things got a little hot. When people disputed with each other at General Conference he would simply say, "We are but brothers, come on brothers," and he'd calm the atmosphere. He exuded Jesus; he carried the presence of God with him. He died during my first term in Kenley Bible College. Probably most of the teaching in my home assembly came from Tommy John Griffiths, a man who was prepared to give his time to young people. When I finished my homework during that little period of time before I went to Kenley, he would be willing and happy for me to go to his home and spend a couple of hours teaching me the Word of God. Fortunately he lived just four or five houses away from where my home was, so I could slip round, and there I was grounded in the Word of God, by a mighty man of God. He knew the Bible, a great teacher of the Word. These men had never been to Bible school, but they had a great knowledge of God's Word. I learned so much in the early days from them. Most of our training was done in the open air. My Uncle Alwyn invariably led the open-air meetings. We had about three a week and on every street corner in the village and surrounding villages we would proclaim Jesus. We would be given about two minutes' notice. You're on next, he'd point to you and then out you went and shared the Gospel. Great training days. Perhaps the earliest recollection I have of taking part in a church service was when I was about five or six years of age, when the youth were taking a meeting in the Salvation Army Citadel in Aberaman, and I was part of the singing group. We first recited, "Hold the fort for I am coming." A great old hymn – we would recite a verse and then sing it. I've often wondered if I ever made hell tremble as a little boy saying, "Hold the fort for I am coming." I think we're a bit more positive now and we're looking forward to the wonderful end, the glorious end of the Church when it will be presented to Jesus by His Father, a glorious conquering, victorious Church. We're on the winning side. And so as part of our training on youth weekends, probably one weekend a month, there again would be opportunities for testimonies and singing. Great times. Many youth rallies with plenty of opportunities. And although you might have made a mess of things you were helped, advised, put right and encouraged. My first message was on the cross. I've often felt over the years there's been a little lapse in preaching on the great fundamental truths: the Blood of Christ, Calvary, the Resurrection, the Second Coming of Christ. They don't seem to be preached about so much these days. We didn't go many weeks without preaching on the cross, the training was invaluable, the teaching tremendous, and opportunities plentiful. However there was a great hill to climb before I entered into Bible college.

I was very much in love with Sylvia Weare, who was from Risca. Her mum and dad were in pastoral ministry for many years in the Cardiff Assembly of God. What an example and what an inspiration in my life. They were a great help to me, and I was deeply in love with their daughter, Sylvia. I had to have a serious talk with Sylvia. I had to tell her that my life was being lived for the glory of God and I'd had a call to the ministry, and as far as the future was concerned it was so uncertain I could not make any plans or any promises regarding developments, because I had to see how God would lead me. Sylvia said she was so happy that I felt that way, and God was first in both our lives. She'd often seen her mum and dad pray and weep together. She's told me many times she would be upstairs listening to them and that she sought to take them as her example. There was a time when she said, "Lord, I want to serve you at the side of someone like my dad," and in the fullness of time that came to be. What a great support they were to us. Many times I preached in Cardiff where I had great opportunities. My father-in-law very generously donated so many books from his library, and the help and encouragement that we had was something that I shall never be able to really thank them for both now and in the Glory. But I thank God for every memory of them and every word of encouragement received from them.

CHAPTER TWO

Leaving home for Bible college

At 16 receiving the call of God and seeking to gain entrance into Bible college, but being told I was far too young, meant agonising months of waiting. But eventually, by persistently 'knocking on the door', I gained entrance into Kenley Bible College. A letter came and I was accepted at 17½. Just before my 18th birthday I left home and went to Kenley. I'd never been away from home before. One can imagine the difficulties, but the distinct call of God was upon my life and with the tremendous support of my parents and the prayer support of my church I went to Kenley. I was the youngest student ever to go into Kenley. Donald Gee was the Principal and one of the founders and pioneering men of Assemblies of God in Great Britain. My time in Bible college was intensive but enjoyable. Because I was so young, and had left school not long ago, I was still in the studying mode, and because of this it made things far easier for me than for those who were easily in their 30s and 40s. In fact, at examination time, I was never lower than third out of all the students in the college and more often than not I was in top place. I was able to use my memory to a great advantage. Some of the tutors were very methodical and very analytical in their presentation of the Word of God. This suited me. I could remember the headings, the sub-headings, and the Scriptures. Particularly from Mr Woodford for he loved this and gave you top marks if you were on the same wavelength as him. Elisha Thompson was resident at the college. A man of God, a man of faith, a man of humility, a man who never sought prominence, he lived in the Old Testament, he knew it, he was there, a magnificent Old Testament teacher. Donald Gee, practical, specialised in pastoral and practical subjects – a great Bible college principal. What I found was that these men lived by faith as we as students lived by faith. They had no salary; they had to trust God as we trusted God. This brought an atmosphere of faith and a great pioneering spirit into the students; to be invited to a church with half a dozen people was like being given a million pounds. The atmosphere at the college was imbibed by us and we longed to get out there and just serve the Lord Jesus Christ. I don't think we looked for the salary, we just wanted the opportunity. Of course there are things that one has learned over the years that were rather silly, which were told to us by certain people. For instance: "You don't take a day off a week. You're serving the Lord and there's no time off when you serve the Lord." A day off would have been good for me and would have saved me a lot of heartaches and problems later on in life. "You don't have to take out a pension; Jesus is coming soon." That too has had its effect upon my life. "Man will never walk on the moon," but we have seen him walk on the moon. And any prognostications, any date setting, any bold statements of that nature need to be carefully analysed. In fact I would say that for leaders today it would be a wise thing to think of having a pension policy. To consider having an early retirement option therein, not necessarily going to 65 years of age, because one never knows the future. Yes, I do believe that Jesus is coming soon, but His Word teaches us wisdom too.

In Bible college I attained the position of Head Student at a very young age. The advantage was that the head student had his own room with his own toilet facility – a great blessing at Kenley. I managed somehow to avoid doing the gardening which, apart from being cold, was hard work – and I don't like gardening; and more often than not I managed to get into the basement peeling the potatoes as an early morning duty – not a bad job on a cold morning because it was nice and warm down in the basement. We got up to some pranks of course, because we had a variety of students with different personalities and different temperaments. I do remember, and I've since apologised to Elwyn Philips, that around the 5th November, when he was in the toilet with the door locked, we put some fireworks through the gap at the top of the door. These were in those days called 'jacky jumpers'. The more he shrieked the more we laughed. Mrs Wright was the matron and, being slightly deaf, she also experienced our pranks. We would set alarm clocks, hidden in the study room, to go off every few minutes. The students would be giggling and laughing and she would not know what was happening. She was a very self-conscious lady and thought we were laughing because something was not right with her clothing or the way she looked.

Sylvia and I got engaged some time after I'd been in Kenley. We were probably a little bit young. I thought: how am I going to go about this buying of the ring? Somehow I managed to save some money and the ring cost £19. This was a lot of money at that time, and certainly a lot of money for me. I had no bank account, so I decided the best thing to do was to go to the Bank of England, with whom at that time you could get an account. After much discussion and investigation I had a brand new chequebook, but only ever used it once when we went to a jewellers in Cardiff. I wrote out the cheque for the engagement ring, and we were then officially engaged. The chequebook was destroyed, there was no more money in it, and no more money to put into it, and so it was really just for that one occasion.

I remember the time when Billy Graham came to England. He was a preacher that all of us admired. He was a man that always looked immaculate in the way he dressed. These were indelible points written into our lives. He used to wear a light grey hat with a large brim, and he would have a light cream raincoat; of course I had to save all my money and buy the same. I remember going to Croydon from Bible college and buying this raincoat and this hat. Now I was only about eight stone in weight, and I was rather gaunt and thin. In fact I used to pray to put on weight. And the gentleman advised me that this hat was very unsuitable for me, but I insisted on having the one with the large brim. One good thing came out of it: the next time I was going home at half term, travelling down by train from Paddington Station and being met by Sylvia at Newport or Cardiff, I had my head out of the window looking for her on the platform and had on this hat with a large brim. She immediately saw me; it was the hat she saw first that stood out and it was a joyous occasion. All through the time in Bible school we prayed for each other, sought God, and looked to Him for what would happen when I came out. Bible school taught us discipline. It was a test of our love for each other and yet we never wavered in our loyalty. There were occasions that were rather humorous too, of course. A time when one would go out preaching on Sundays and come back rather late by train, underground, and we would have supper which was usually very thick sandwiches, very basic, and soup that would be kept in a vacuum flask. The soup didn't keep too well in the flask, but we would be very hungry when we came home so we would either endure or enjoy the soup; the sandwiches were too overpowering by that time. On this occasion my friend and I decided we would have to dispose of these sandwiches – wisely, because they must not be found, otherwise we would certainly have to meet with Matron. So George Davis and I decided we would take a walk outside the college, down the lane, which had thick hedges on both sides, and we would hide the sandwiches in a paper bag in the bushes, hopefully not to be seen again. That was the end of it. We went to bed and forgot all about the incident until the next day, after dinner, when the matron, Mrs Wright, asked for Mr Davis and Mr Hanford to come to her room immediately after lunch. We had forgotten what had happened and had no idea why we were to meet until we went into this room and saw this magnificent, highly polished round table where our sandwiches were displayed on newspaper. What had happened to the sandwiches which should have rotted in the hedge?

Someone had evidently seen us do the deed and 'grassed' on us. We could do nothing except repent and take the punishment: a whole week cleaning potatoes in the kitchen and extra work in the garden. It seemed like further punishment when part of our training was how to fold the tablecloths properly and how to lay the tables with every piece of cutlery in their right place. There was the practical side and the staff at Kenley Bible College were so dedicated and were only there for our good, I feel sure. During our time in Kenley some of us were also part of the Revivaltime broadcasting team who regularly, once every week or two weeks, would make our way to Bromley Assembly where the programmes would be recorded. It was a good day out for us. We used to go to a restaurant for dinner, which was quite a nice change, and of course we met a lot of friends there. I was part of the Revivaltime Quartet made up of friends Desmond Evans, Alan Hocking, Glyn Thomas, Phil Cochrane, Douglas Bean and that brilliant pianist, Edwin Holland. It did change occasionally. When it came to end of term we had to find replacements for those leaving, but most of us were together for the majority of the time. This meant as well, of course, that we did go around the country to rallies and conventions and so we did have an opportunity to have a break from Bible college. In fact, when we first started, Desmond Evans was the leader of the Revivaltime Choir that met on the same day. John Nelson Parr was the preacher. Keith Munday followed him and there were two or three other preachers over the years. And then eventually, as part of my ministry, I came into broadcasting and had the opportunity of sharing the Gospel as well. Douglas Quy who was then pastoring in the area was very much in charge of the Revivaltime programme, a very gifted and capable man who was very kind to us. He was good at teaching and training and the Bromley Assembly so frequently opened the door of hospitality to us, as we sought to share the Gospel. We also took part in programmes on different radio stations apart from Radio Luxemburg, but Radio Luxemburg was the main station. It cost a hundred pounds for every half hour broadcast, which was a lot of money in the 1950s. But God supplied all that was needed. In fact there was a time when we broadcast on Radio Caroline which was an offshore ship, anchored outside territorial waters, in the south of England. There was a lot of discussion about that because some considered it was illegal broadcasting, so it didn't last too long.

More about my broadcasting ministry later...

Many of those who left the college at that time are still serving the Lord in the work of God throughout the world after many years. The Bible college is no longer at Kenley; it has been transferred to Mattersey near Doncaster. However, memories are still very fresh and there have been times recently when I have been in that area, and have driven up Kenley Lane, only to see that new buildings have been built on the site. It is a memorable spot for me, for that was a place where, for two-and-a-half years, I not only learned the Scriptures, but I learned how to live and how to move in the power of God's Spirit. We were privileged to sit at the feet of men like Harold Horton, men on fire for God, men who inspired faith, men who taught you how to move in the Gifts of the Spirit. There were many setbacks that I had to face, even in Bible college with peritonitis. What is the answer to sickness? Why didn't Jesus heal me? God put into my soul some steel and some strength. God was saying, there's going to be hills, all kinds of difficulties, and one is sickness, but it must never hold you back. You face it and Jesus can heal you or take you through it, that's a big lesson to learn! Even if you go God's way everything's not going to work out just as you want it to. If you follow the will of God there's going to be upsets and hardships, but I tell you what, you'll never be satisfied by doing anything else but following God's plan for your life. I left Kenley with my certificate and a gold diploma. Some people don't like diplomas or degrees, and there's no doubt others place more importance on them than they should, but as a mark of your achievement they're very pleasurable to look at and they're a reminder of the time spent preparing for the ministry in Kenley. The principles learned in Bible school are still with me today, but you never stop learning, especially the principles of discipline in study and in prayer. Those were the days when of course you had to preach Sunday morning, Sunday night, probably at Bible study in the week and maybe a short word at prayer time. You had to get disciplined before God and wait upon God until you got something from Him. It was tough, but it never did us any harm. The Word tells us to: "Study to show yourself approved unto God". Set your times before God, and if the alarm goes, or the front door bell goes, or the telephone rings, your time before God is the priority.

Two poems by Joan Nichols, Bolton Pentecostal Church

Who's bashing you over the head today,
Who's having a bit of a go?
It isn't Me, 'cos Terry, you're My child
And I love you so.
You open up My Word,
You help My people understand,
And you never attempt to do it,
Without first taking hold of My hand.
You offer Me your heart,
You're willing to change,
To do things new,
And people see the beauty and the love I've placed in you.
You're real, no airs and graces,
Overflowing with warmth and joy,
Can't you see on their faces,
How they love the 'little boy'
Within the Godly teacher,
Respected, loved and anointed,
They know you've met with Me
And bring the things I want to say
At the appointed time.

That's why you're special and precious,
Child of Mine.
Keep on doing, Terry,
For I have more to impart to thee,
Carry on, but Hey! Before you do...
Pass the head basher over to Me.

What a mighty man of God,
What a joy, Oh what delight,
To hear you open up the Word of God the other night,
I just had to write to say
That I went home encouraged and blessed,
Thinking how much I appreciate a man who gives his best,
Who takes the time to get with God
In Prayer and in His Word.
Then shares, with such sincerity, the truth of what he's heard,
And the way you shared your struggles,
In an honest, open way,
Gave me the courage to press on with 'mine' another day.
So what is it I'm saying?
I can go on and on once I start.
Well, Terry, just wanted to share the big 'Thanks',
That today God stirred up in my heart.

CHAPTER THREE

Peterborough, here I come at 20 years of age

Coming to the end of my time at Bible college in Kenley there was the anxious but prayerful time of wanting to know what God was going to lead me into when I left the college. At that time there were very few opportunities to work alongside an experienced man which would have been the ideal. So one was thrust into a pastoral situation with theory learned at college but the practical side of looking after people was very sparse. I was nevertheless so grateful to God for opening up the assembly at Peterborough in Northamptonshire where, in the summer of 1957, just a month or two after leaving Kenley, I was installed as Pastor. It was a fairly new building, but the church had been going for some time. At that particular time the oversight was made up of elderly men but they were looking for a younger man as Pastor. Well, I was just 20 years of age. The two elders in the church at that time, as was the custom, sat on the platform during the services. Soon I found that these men often nodded off to sleep during the meetings – either it was my boring preaching or their age that caused this. I did mention on one occasion, in one of my sermons, that during the olden days in the Anglican Church the 'Sidesmen' had long poles with a knob on the end whereby they would go up and down the aisles and stretch across the row, and anyone going to sleep would be awakened. On my way out that night, one of the stewards said, "Pastor, you would only have needed a very short pole tonight." Both the brothers had been asleep behind me. Great inspiration for a young man starting in his first pastorate! Nevertheless, they were good, consistent and faithful men. Peterborough had about 30 members. A nice building, small with a lawn around it, which was kept immaculately.

Regularly a big night for many young people was when the latest sensation was in town. On one occasion it was the pop star Terry Dene. Hundreds of young people were queuing to get into the large theatre, and here was I, cycling to the prayer meeting, where about 15 people would meet. I was a little jealous. However the day came when Terry Dene became a Christian. I met him and related about the time we both were in Peterborough but for different purposes. For that first year I lived at 48 Eastgate in Peterborough. A widow by the name of Mrs Payne looked after me very well. She was very pleased when I did get married as the first thing she told my wife was, "I loved having your husband stay with me, but he is so difficult to feed and lived on chicken and peas." I think she taught me some lessons and she did manage to get me eating some things that I had not eaten before. It was a great day when Sylvia came back with me to Peterborough, as my wife, and we lived at 28 Granville Street. The church had bought this house and we lived happily there for just over three years. Sylvia soon got involved in the church, in the children's work, youth work, open-air work and I think in every other bit of work the church was involved in. We were so happy to be together. Just a week or two after we were married it was Sylvia's 21st birthday, and in those days everyone did something special when one was 21. I wanted to do likewise, but as my salary was only five pounds per week I could not buy or arrange anything special for my dear wife. However God provided in an unusual way. Sylvia put on a coat that she had not worn for some considerable time and we decided to take a walk in the park. While walking through the park, her hand was in her pocket and she was surprised to find a ten-shilling note. That was a wonderful discovery to us. We went to the first shop, bought some sweets and chocolates and enjoyed them in the park. That was her special 21st birthday present. I cannot really say from me, but God had provided. Oftentimes our special moment to look forward to in the week was when we could save a penny or two to buy sticks of liquorice. That was a highlight of the week.

But God blessed us in that home and eventually supplied us with a car. It was a Hillman Minx and came from Sylvia's cousin. To us it was like owning a Rolls Royce. In fact I thought I would make it look better by painting the inside of the car a bright yellow. It didn't go down too well, either with my wife or anyone else. The first trip we took in this car was to Leicester but it broke down in the middle of that very busy city. We had some good friends in Peterborough, and Mr Wilshaw, who looked after us so well, came out to Leicester and towed us back home, and we got the car repaired and eventually changed to something a little better. Up to that time, of course, we had to rely on bicycles. Fortunately that part of the country is rather flat and we did not have too many mountains or hills to climb. But distances were quite substantial. On one occasion, after cycling out for a meeting in one of the neighbouring villages, we left it a little late in coming home. We had to ride back in the dark and there was not too much lighting about. It was quite frightening. But again, it was an experience that we have in our memory.

There was a time when I had to stop for toilet purposes and I left my bicycle outside. When I came out I was horrified to find a herd of cattle, which were not being controlled very well, trampling over my bicycle. I ran after the farmer and demanded that he do something about it. I did get some new tyres and wheels for my bicycle. We were glad when the bicycle era came to an end and God blessed us with four wheels rather than two. Many times we saw the church full to capacity. We had many outreaches, both in the building and in other halls in the town. The people were forward-looking and we were so glad that many people came to know Jesus as Saviour and Lord at that time. A lot of work was done in the open air and a lot was done in the parks with outreaches of various kinds. We were being well prepared in dealing with different types of people. Mr and Mrs Allen came to us from the Salvation Army and were great workers in the church. Mr Allen accepted the work of the Holy Spirit more easily than his wife. He did have a squeaky, high-pitched voice and on one occasion he called out the number of a hymn he wished us to sing. I didn't quite hear the number or recognise who shouted the number out, so I asked, "Would that sister please repeat the number again?" To my embarrassment Mr Allen repeated the number. On another occasion, at a prayer meeting where we all knelt down to pray, the couple were kneeling behind us. Mr Allen constantly spoke in other tongues and his wife would try and restrain him. To stop him this time we saw her take a chunk of his rear end and to the amazement of all present, in the middle of speaking in tongues, we heard a loud, "Ouch!"

Things were difficult financially. On one occasion we were blessed with a group of Americans coming in from one of the USAF camps not too far away from Peterborough. It was obviously their practice, in their home churches in America, to give their tithes directly to the minister. This was the minister's salary; offerings were given separately for the maintenance of the church building etc. On this occasion the amount of the offering was announced and it was quite high for us, and on the way out one American brother said to me, "Well, Pastor, I am so glad that you did so well last week with the offering."

Astounded, I asked, "What do you mean?"

He said, "Well, the offering was a good one and evidently you were blessed."

I said, "No. I would receive the same whatever the offering was." He was disturbed by this, as he knew that five pounds was not doing much for us. From that time on, this particular brother would bless us by supplementing my income with personal gifts.

We certainly learned a lot of lessons in those early days, and some hard ones too. Lessons on how to look after people and how fickle people can be. I remember times when there would be a lot of arguments over what colour jellies the ladies should make at convention time. If one person made a yellow jelly last year, it had to be a yellow jelly this year. If someone else dared to take their colour, people were not too happy. There were times when we had some people who wanted to disturb us. There was one woman who came into the church and, during prayer time, would speak in tongues and then begin to swear. We had enough of this and Sylvia and I determined that this was not to continue. We went to one of the brothers who did not want a confrontation. We waited until the end of the meeting and then tackled this woman and said that we could not have this in the House of God. Whereupon she shrieked at such a pitch that Sylvia literally left the ground. She just went up and when she came down onto 'terra firma' again, she gently enquired, "Who are you shouting at? You don't frighten me." The woman left the church and we did not see her in church again. But that same woman used to come to our house and come around the back way, oftentimes to the windows and make funny noises and scary faces at us. Whenever there was a guest preacher she would be a nuisance. There was a time, we were told, when she came to the house where Donald Gee was staying during a convention at our church. Donald had enough of her disturbances in the night. He put up the window and he had a bucket of water which he tipped over her to get rid of her. On a number of occasions she came and pushed her mother's false teeth through our letterbox. This type of incident was part and parcel of our training in looking after people of all sorts. But then it is our privilege to care for the flock of God, to guard them and to teach them very important lessons.

We had twins in the church: Shirley and June. These fine, loyal young women invited us to supper one night. They invited us to meet and pray for their parents before we started the meal. They took us upstairs where we found two lumps in bed under some sacking as blankets. We duly prayed, without any heads appearing from under the clothes! The girls had prepared salmon sandwiches, which I am sure cost them dearly. I resisted as much as I could, but Sylvia was more polite than me, although it cost her a night of asthma which we shall never forget. We could barely see through the thick air, caused partly by the ashes from the coal fire being swept into the corner of the room.

On another occasion it was a great encouragement to be invited out for a meal by a couple who had good jobs and a large house – we looked forward to it so much. When we arrived our expectations were not dampened. The large, highly polished table was immaculately laid with silver cutlery. It looked as if a banquet was going to take place. We were hungry for we had missed our lunch in anticipation. Our places were taken at the table and we waited for the lids to be taken off the impressive, large, silver tureens that duly appeared. Imagine our disappointment and amazement when the lids were lifted off to reveal a rather small pork pie which would be divided between the four of us. A small salad and little else completed the meal. To add to the disastrous event, the man of the house suggested that it might have been more in order to have had a prayer meeting and a time of fasting. The latter I think had already been arranged! We couldn't laugh then, but we did on our way home. I thought I had enough money to take some fish and chips home but I didn't, so we prolonged the fast.

I guess that the main hill that we had to encounter in Peterborough, our first church, was the fact that we were so young and inexperienced and we were taught the hard way. It was the hill of dependency on older brethren to give us advice and help us which did not happen. The best way to be trained is face-to-face with men who have been through the trials. The theory of books is not so effective as the experience of men. Another hill, of course, was trusting God for finance. Those were very difficult and hard days. For most of our ministry, Sylvia worked. She took employment to help. This blessed us in so many different ways. These days and years, the very first of our married life and ministry, were tough, but God never failed. He taught us how to budget, how to discipline our finances and how to trust God, and it has held us in good stead for the remainder of our ministry.

CHAPTER FOUR

All shipshape and Bristol fashion

After three-and-a-half years we were called to Trinity Tabernacle in Bristol. We were following a fine old timer, Pastor Mitchell. This was quite an upheaval for us, leaving our first church. We had not stayed too long, but long enough to become Secretary of the District Council and deeply involved in the administration of the district. In fact it was the beginning of many years of holding most of the posts and offices in what was then the district council, chairman of several councils and committees and a member of national bodies in the fellowship as well. It all started at Peterborough, the hill of inexperience. The hill of trusting God. God never fails. So packing up all that we had and moving to Bristol was quite an event. This was a big change for us as we were now going to a larger church, a larger building and maybe in some ways a greater historical past. We also encountered the difficulty of following an older man. We were not sure whether he wanted to retire or not. However, this was soon overcome and we settled in well.

The other problem was where were we going to live? The church had planned to arrange accommodation for us but this fell through at the last minute. We were very kindly accommodated by the secretary and his wife, Hedley and Margaret Excell and their children. They provided us with tremendous hospitality. While we desperately wanted our own place we were so happy that we were well looked after. We did have some great long times of prayer at night. Hedley insisted on praying around the world, and we knelt down by our chairs before we went to rest. Probably there were times when Sylvia and I were so tired that we would have a nap in-between the long prayers. However the Hedleys were great friends to us and Margaret was also a great cook. Then came a day when we saw a house for sale. In fact, it was right opposite where we were living with Mr and Mrs Excell, and it was £1,500. A lot of money to us. A deposit had to be placed of £150. Of course we did not have the deposit. We prayed: "Lord, if this is your will, please help us in some wonderful way." Through shortness of time we could not do too much searching around or asking. The day came when the offer had to be made and the deposit put on the table. We came home from visiting and there, on the table in Mr and Mrs Excell's room, was an envelope that we were told contained a cheque for £150. We were never to ask where the money came from and we do not know to this day. However, that was the beginning of the purchase of our home on Greenbank Road in Eastville, Bristol. God had wonderfully supplied. For a time, to supplement our income, I took a job collecting coal money from people who paid for their fuel with weekly amounts. This took about two hours early each morning, for three or four days a week. My boss was Pastor Wreyford, an AoG minister in the city.

One of our saddest experiences was when Tony Payne died in his late teens with leukaemia. Tony went into Bible school after beginning a promising career in a lucrative trade. He also had trials for Bristol City Football Club and for others. He was a fine athlete and a promising preacher. During one summer holiday between Bible school terms, in order to save some money, he took a job in a butchers. Tony accidentally cut into his thigh, but he took little notice until he felt the blood flowing down his leg. He was rushed into hospital. While he was there, he was diagnosed as being seriously ill with leukaemia and later died. This shook us immensely.

On the humorous side, one of our older believers did

not like mice, but neither did I especially. When Mrs Rampling rang me at 2am, pleading for me to visit and deal with a mouse, off I went praying – and I thanked God when I arrived and the mouse had escaped!

While we were in Bristol both of our children were born. First Sharon in 1961 and Jason a little later, in 1965. They were a great blessing to us and we had a fine doctor there who was a brethren man, a wonderful Christian who looked after us so well. We had many happy days in Bristol. It is a very fine city. The fellowship among the assemblies was great because there were probably at least twelve Assemblies of God in and around Bristol. They were good men, varied men with different kinds of personalities. Men like Ernie Crewe, who became a great friend of mine, Alfred Missen at the Mount of Olives and other men. Ministry opportunities came thick and fast. I can recollect now outstanding conventions held all over the country. Certain ones stand out. Newton Abbott, Glynneath, Dundonald and Letterkenny, to name a few. I was kept very busy in the church as we were a very 'go ahead' evangelistic church, and so many came to know the Lord Jesus Christ weekly and from a number of crusades. It was called Trinity Tabernacle, and if you imagine a tabernacle being like the one in the Old Testament or Spurgeon's Tabernacle in London, our church building was completely different from any of these. It was situated in the middle of a busy street, adjacent to some shops and run-down premises. But it was the Tabernacle where we met with God and we had some great times there. Some outstanding moments come fresh into my mind. There was a time when an American evangelist, T L Osborne, visited Britain, and one of the number of nationwide centres he visited for a crusade was the Colston Hall in Bristol. Mr Osborne followed the same procedure when asking for financial support in each venue in the UK. God had told him to do the same thing wherever he went, although we thought this was special to us in Bristol. Forty chairs were placed across the platform and 40 people were encouraged to bring their £100 offering and sit on a chair. Cheques or IOUs would be accepted, the latter under 'oath'. I was amazed to see six members of our church go to fill seats. What amazed me more was that most of them were receiving church support for clothes and food; some were new converts from a life of prostitution. I doubted that all six had £100 between them, and wasn't our church loaded with debt? As a young pastor it hurt. My wife and I worked to make enough for our own needs because the church's salary was so low. However, positive lessons were being taught to me. If Mr Osborne needed that amount of money, he had a right to ask for it. It stimulated my faith to stop being afraid and to be bold for God's work. I left the meeting with a thankful heart. The meetings proceeded, some people were saved, and one or two came into the church. In fact the next Sunday the campaign manager, a man by the name of M E Hayes, came to the meeting. I invited him onto the platform and quite suddenly, unpremeditated, although I knew that we were in desperate need of an electric organ, I said, "We could get an electric organ by next Sunday if 20 people gave £20." In a matter of seconds, 20 people jumped up and said that they would do it. We had the electric organ by the following week. So I was helped, stirred and maybe taught from these men some of the positive issues. In fact, Mr Hayes was the first to stand up. We did see many blessings from that, as some people said that we should not have gone for an organ but we should have gone for the debt that was on the church. I felt a bit critical and very hurt over this. So I said that maybe those who don't feel like giving to the organ would like to make a contribution to the church debt. In a matter of weeks every need was met. The debt of the church was cleared and we pressed on with evangelism. God is good. The lesson learned here was that the hills of difficulty in financial restraint, and holding back God's work, can be overcome by simple faith: knowing God's will, asking in God's way and asking in faith and believing that He will reward us. Among the six who went to the platform to promise £100 was a prostitute, a young mother with six children from different fathers but wonderfully saved, and she became a tremendous witness for Jesus. We told her not to return home by her usual route which was through the area where she used to ply her trade. But she didn't listen. She said, "I'll go back that way. I'll meet my friends and I'll tell them what Christ has done in my life." She did that and amazingly and unto the glory of God some of her friends came to know the Lord Jesus as Saviour and Lord. Shortly after the crusade letters came from the evangelist asking for the payment of IOUs. I wrote to him saying there was little possibility that one or two could fulfil the promise. Letters came back pronouncing judgement on such folk for breaking their vows.

We also had a crusade with Peter Scothern. Peter was quite well known throughout the movement at that time and had been used of God in many parts of the country, especially in Scotland.

Some funny incidents happened here, too. At that time many pastors insisted on ladies wearing hats – that included Sylvia, who rather enjoyed wearing them. She was quite proud of her hats and she saw that many who came out for prayer fell down under the power of God's Spirit. This was not for her, especially with a hat on. However, she was very distressed with hay fever. She stood at the back of the church one night. Well, you can guess what happened. Without hands being laid on her, down she went under the power of God. The hat left her head and rolled down the centre of the aisle, which at that time did not have any carpet laid, just like a penny rolling from the back of the building to the front. It may have dealt with a bit of pride, I am not sure. But God met with her, and I am glad to say that – although there were some temporary problems when she threw all her tablets in the waste bin and during the night had a bad attack and rescued them again – God answered prayer and, soon afterwards, God delivered her from the tablets and healed her by the power of the Spirit. Our first child was just six weeks old and Sylvia was caring for her 24 hours a day. The tablets made Sylvia sleepy and she feared she would drop our daughter, so the matter was quite important to us.

Again people came into the church. We had the joy of seeing our neighbours, Den and Mavis, come to the Lord. It did take a bit of socialising and playing of Monopoly with them but, to Sylvia's surprise, one day Den jumped over the back wall and asked, "What must I do to be saved?" So, taken aback, Sylvia told him to wait for me to come home, but meanwhile let's have a prayer about it. Everything is solved by "let's pray over it".

Numbers came in to the church to see what God was doing. Of course, you always have the good and the bad. We had one man who came in and, publicly, while I was stood on the platform, rebuked me from the congregation and said that he was the chosen man to be pastor of this church and that he was John the Baptist. I asked him to leave and some stewards assisted him outside. When he was outside, he pronounced a curse on the church and said that no souls would ever be saved in that church and that God would deal with me in drastic ways. Thankfully, the precious blood of Jesus protected me. Mr and Mrs Ron McCatty came in from the Plymouth Brethren. Ron was a black brother and his wife was from Wales; they became good friends of ours. In fact they knew some of my family. Ron was very keen to be baptised in the Holy Spirit, so the first opportunity that came I prayed for him and Jesus granted his desire. The only problem was that his wife rang me during the week, very disturbed, saying, "He has not stopped talking in tongues for three days and three nights. He cannot work, he cannot do anything in the house. He has just been worshipping, praying and praising for three days and three nights." That's the first time I have been asked to go and pray that someone might stop speaking in tongues. God wonderfully used Ron. He became a fine member of our church and, more recently, the great Elim church in Bristol. He wrote the foreword for a book concerning the life of Ron Jones, who spent many fruitful years in the Elim Church as a pastor. Ron McCatty was a manipulative therapist, a very clever man who helped a lot of people, one being my wife, when she suffered with a locked jaw. And he had his own rather unusual but successful treatment working on her as soon as we paid a visit to them.

And so the work built up. We had our difficulties with

personalities, and also in understanding different cultures, for Bristol is a very cosmopolitan city and our church was made up of many cultures. It didn't help when people from different countries and traditions got married and all the bridesmaids came dressed in the same colour as the bride, and there always seemed to be so many of them in the main wedding group. One fine young Christian asked me to conduct his wedding but his bride would only arrive in the UK a very short time before the big day. I arranged the wedding details in good faith. Imagine my despair when a short time after the event he knocked on my door requesting that I dedicate the baby, which incidentally was not his. I did think the bride was looking an unusual shape on her wedding day!

There were strong personalities to deal with and one or two problems when marriages broke up, which is something that we have had to face over the years and which still breaks our hearts, especially when some of the people involved tell you lies to your face. I would rather hear bad news but it be the truth, than an attempt to cover things up. We got through those problems and baptised many people in water and saw many filled with the Spirit and healed after prayer. One young man was instantly healed of a large hernia, yet I had to go into hospital for surgery for the same thing. I remember collapsing on the platform with kidney stones and being taken into hospital. However, God gave us a great band of praying people and we would meet in the vestry very early on Saturday mornings and pray God's blessing on the church. I feel that we had a very fruitful ministry in Bristol. People came into the church. There were not many Sunday evenings that we preached the Gospel when people were not saved. Whilst we were there we drew up plans for a new building. We paved the way for a new building and then eventually, after I had left Bristol, it was erected on a roundabout in a very strategic position not far from where we were, and the work of God went on, albeit not an Assembly of God.

The Kingdom of God is what we build with God's help and I learned in Bristol that the benefits of fellowship, the benefits of meeting other men and learning from them, was so helpful. I also gained experience by visiting smaller churches where there was no particular Holy Spirit atmosphere. I learned early on that you must carry your own fire with you. Fire in the belly will cause the message to be effective. So many men are determined to work up an atmosphere these days. We need to call down the power of God's Spirit and when that atmosphere prevails, God does things.

I was so happy to widen my experience in ministry around the country and especially with friends around the area of Bristol. I remember going to an induction service at Ivy Church and being introduced as Tony Hancock, not Terry Hanford. I guess the minister had been looking at television fairly recently before that particular induction service. Something else began while I was at Bristol. I was invited to help with the arrangements for the Full Gospel Businessmen's Fellowship World Conference in the Royal Albert Hall in London. It was a huge venture and hundreds went from the area. As a result I had a letter from the Secretary inviting me to New York to preach at one of their conventions as a kind of 'thank you' for the work I had done. That was all arranged in Bristol. I felt that the best thing to do was to get a young man from Bible school to come and take the church over for the couple of weeks. Eventually, David Skelton came from the Bible college and did a wonderful job of looking after the church. Not only that, he did find his future wife from Malmesbury, a town not too far away from Bristol. David and I have been good friends over the years. He found a wonderful wife and we had links with the church there during the early days. We travelled to Malmesbury for conventions and mini-crusades to help the work and David did a marvellous job. It helped him in his calling to the work of God because, while at Bible college, you always long for the experience of being out on the field, in the church looking after people rather than learning all the theory about church growth. We were so blessed when two families from West Bromwich moved to our area – at last we had some top class musicians. Eventually, when an opportunity came to plant a church in Yate, these families took a leading part and Ivor

Chadd became the first pastor. To pioneer and hold marches and open-air meetings in Yate was great experience. Tommy Tucker, Ivor's father-in-law, was a unique man – a bare fist boxer in his early days but wonderfully saved in prison, and he had an outstanding memory of the Bible. He invariably helped every preacher if they stumbled on a quote or reference. He also moved from the back to the front of church if the preacher warmed up. His encouragement vocally and in action was unique. I appreciated that man.

CHAPTER FIVE

Devon cream teas and violets

The time came for us to be disturbed again and to move on by the prompting of God's Spirit. God gave me a call to Exeter, a beautiful part of the country. It seems that each time God was good in moving us from one good place to another. I was heading for Exeter but Sylvia had to stay behind until our house had been sold. When we put the house up for sale, we encountered a difficulty which we never anticipated. We found that there was subsidence in the property and none of the potential buyers could secure a mortgage for it. The only answer was that God would provide somebody who was a 'cash buyer' who would be able to put the house right. We prayed. Sylvia went through agony caring for our two children on her own in addition to this problem without my help in Bristol. I was staying long weekends in Exeter and coming back to Bristol for a day or two in the middle of the week. God was good. He sent a man along who was a builder and eventually he bought the property and was able to put right the things that it needed. Of course we did not gain so much profit on the house as we would have done but we did have a little.

One of the biggest lessons of our lives was just about to be learned. We had these few hundred pounds to save after the house sale and the debts were paid but we were moving to Exeter actually for less salary. We felt that that we would probably need to have some savings 'up our sleeves' as a second string if we fell on hard times. I saw an advert in the local press for the Guardian Bank, offering high interest. Having little experience of investing money, we should have asked for some advice. We placed the money in that bank. It was registered in the Channel Isles. Some time after we had moved to Exeter we were sitting in a deckchair on the sands in Exmouth for a little break and refreshment. I bought a newspaper and the headline read: 'Guardian Bank gone bust'. My colour changed; Sylvia knew something drastic had happened. The news came out that we had lost our money. A big lesson here: if you are going to trust God and you are saying that you are trusting God without any visible means of support, then you don't have money up your sleeve or stacked away somewhere for a rainy day. It did teach us a big lesson. If you trust in God, you trust in God. If you have got some money spare, well and good but this was the lesson we were taught. Always be completely straight before God.

Our new church was a big old building in Exeter but wonderfully situated near the riverside. It was a rather strange building because it was on two floors. The top floor was our main sanctuary which had the inconvenience of stairs to get to it, or there was a small staircase coming down from a high level street, but not many seemed to use that. A great old building with a great history. We did find in the kitchen, when we were clearing out one day, some plates with the words 'Penny a dinner' on them. Obviously they were used in a past age, probably a hundred years ago when we were told Exe Island was a place where people came who could not afford food and they would be fed at this place. So it had a good history, and indeed we have wonderful memories of that church too. It was there that our daughter, Sharon, was baptised in the Holy Spirit, when David Petts came to minister. It was there that we saw many come to know Christ. Strange things happened in that church. There was a man who always seemed to steal ladies' umbrellas and would walk out of the church with these funny points sticking out through his clothes, which were the ends of the umbrellas. He would always dispute the fact that he had taken anything. One day we read an article about him in the newspaper, that he had emigrated to Australia. He obviously had quite a bit of money and possibly sold those umbrellas towards his cause!

Another gentleman, who always raised his hand during my appeal for people to come to Christ on Sunday night, continued until I asked him, "Why do you do it every time?"

He said, "Well, you see Pastor, you do put your heart into it. You do preach the Gospel with great clarity and great gusto and when people don't put their hand up I feel sorry for you. So I do it." I pointed out to him that it would not matter too much whether his hand was up or not, unless he himself was giving his life to Christ.

We often had waiting meetings when people were filled with the Spirit and there were many people healed and many people saved. I was a good friend of John Cunningham and his father from Haldon Court in Exmouth, who ran a holiday home. John was a good old Pentecostal but was never baptised in the Spirit, and this had become a major problem to him and to many of his friends. For many years he had been prayed for and he had sought earnestly but there seemed to be some block. Eventually, there was a Home Missions Conference in Birmingham and I persuaded John to come with me. John drove and at that conference he was wonderfully filled with the Holy Spirit and spoke in tongues. I believe that was a momentous day in John's life and walk with Jesus. I am so glad that he was filled with the Holy Ghost that day, as it seemed like a 'do or die' situation. This seemed to be John's last opportunity to receive the Holy Spirit. God meets us when we are desperate.

We made a big drive in those days to reach young people, and had the use of a little building on the level opposite our church which was almost like a cave. It was the basement of a three or four-storey older building. We had the vision of adapting this into a coffee bar. It was the age when coffee bars were in vogue. We called it 'Adullam's Cave', for it has connotations from the Old Testament where probably the rogues and rebels and bad people met, maybe quite applicable for us too! It was done out magnificently by some of the young people. By digging and scraping we went right back to the bare stonework and glossed it over. It looked very nice. We opened a coffee bar as a meeting room and a sports place.

The young people of the church did some tremendous decoration and painting. There many unsaved young people were reached for Jesus Christ in a contemporary way, who otherwise would not have been reached. John Tucker, who later moved to Croydon and became a deacon in the church there, was wonderfully gifted with creative ideas. John was a tremendous help during those days, as was Tom Perrier, Roger Blackmore and Marion Hayward. Roger was one of my 'sons' in the Gospel who moved to the United States. I had the joy of leading his mum and dad to Christ while we were in Exeter. His dad was saved in a crusade we held in Crediton. The only one who got saved in that town hall was Roger's dad, and yet he came from Exeter. That was a great joy and we have met up with Roger a number of times since he has been in the United States. When we first met Roger he was a young lad in short trousers and he was quite a podgy little boy. But God has used him greatly and when he met up with Jill at Bible school and they married it was a great day for us. We dedicated their children and had the joy of dedicating their grandchild when we were invited out to the States for that great occasion.

Adullam's cave was a means of reaching young people in the town. We had a varied program every Saturday night, and would number over one hundred every time we met. Sometimes we would go out onto the canal. There we nearly lost one or two lives as young people were tipped out from the canoes and almost drowned, supposedly in fun. But people had to dive in and rescue them. Barbeques out on the Rooks' farms were always a great success. What great days they were, days when a number of people with brethren background came into the church and were filled with the Spirit. John Rook was one, who later became a pastor in Assemblies of God in Dorchester. Behind it all was the vision, the strength and the work of the Bartlett family and of the Haywards, who were great people in the church. It was a great loss to the church generally when Idris Bartlett died suddenly in Dorchester not long after moving from Exeter. His two daughters died at an early age under tragic circumstances, the elder daughter, Heather, having entered God's work and married the pastor of the Dorchester

Assembly, died of cancer. The younger daughter, Ruth, who married into the Anglican Church, died in a car accident. We have admired Gwen Bartlett for the years that she has kept faithful to God and to the work of God in Dorchester.

Exeter was the centre of the South West District Council area. When I became Chairman and Secretary of the district I travelled right down to Cornwall and almost up to Bristol, visiting the pastors and their churches to offer encouragement. Again, ministry widened and this gave me experience as well as looking after the flock of God and seeing it built up. Of course in Exeter there were more hills to get over and mountains to tackle. Some of the major tasks of leadership, I believe, were being moulded into my life. These tasks were: planning, organising, motivating and controlling – not with a heavy hand, but giving direction and leading people, rather than driving them. Leadership begins with the desire to achieve, to raise the standard and attain the goals. Recently I heard about the difficulties in relating to some people that we need to learn in pastoral life. Let the people know what you can do for them. Try to understand them and be a good listener. So many have said that "people don't listen to me". Don't invade people's lives. Be tactful, because we must have respect for the rights, feelings and thoughts of other people. Be honest with people's feelings, and be yourself, take your mask off, and never push a relationship.

In those years in Exeter I believe so many of these excellent leadership principles were woven into my life. There were mountains to get over, mountains I encountered when I was young, of inadequacy, intimidation and sensitivity. All these things God can use, but He toughens us up. He sharpens the edges. Integrity is so important as we face the future and also deal with the past. If you cannot say anything good, don't say anything. If you make a mistake, don't excuse it, evaluate what went wrong, and improve next time. Be flexible, open and don't lose contact with people. These are hills and mountains, which many never learn to scale. If we want to conquer a bigger mountain, if we want to accomplish a bigger task, then we have to be faithful in carrying out God's smaller plans. We must be prepared to be teachable and learn as we are going along.

CHAPTER SIX

No Lord! Not London or Manchester!

Our time in Exeter was a great learning curve in our lives. It held us in good stead for when the next move came from Exeter in a most remarkable way. Really, we were so happy in Exeter. It was a wonderful place to live and we had been there now quite a number of years. I decided that I was going to ask Ernest Anderson, a brother that I had not had much to do with since Bible school days, but whom I knew because he was so well known in the movement. I thought I would ring him and ask if he would come and preach at one of our conventions. When I telephoned him he pulled me up straight away. He said, "I was just going to ring you, Terry. How did you know to ring me ?"

I asked, "What do you mean, how did I know to ring you?"

"Well," he replied, "I was just going to ring you to ask you something."

I said, "Well, look, before we deal with that can I ask you if you will come to this convention?"

He said, "Just a minute. Hold that. God has very definitely told me that I am to ask you if you will consider coming to Denton Assembly in Manchester, to pastor this church."

God had revealed this to us. So, after quite some procedures and remarkable callings and movements of God, it came to pass. It was a hard and difficult time for us. The night I handed in my resignation was a weeknight when we were baptising 17 people who had come to know Christ. It was a great night of highs in God, of exaltation and praise, and I felt that I wanted to stay in Exeter forever. But the call of God to move on was beginning to disturb me. So much so, that I thought that I should at least go up and meet the folk in Denton. But I was so disinterested that I didn't even ask Sylvia to come with me. I thought, well, I'll go out of courtesy. God had given me a Scripture from Isaiah: "God will remove all the mountains and difficulties and He will make a plain path for me." When I arrived at the house I was staying at in Denton, with Mr and Mrs Dawson, the Scripture that God had given me was the same as the Scripture on the wall in their living room. I began to feel shaky inside and thought, 'God, are you really beginning something here?' That was the start of our move from Exeter to Denton. Again we had difficulties with property.

We were on our way to Denton to live temporarily in the church manse. The Exeter Assembly had benefited, thankfully, because the sale of the church manse meant quite an increase in profit but we were on low money and had no equity. We landed in Denton with very little money, and lived in the church manse, which was quite a nice home with high ceilings and big rooms, but very cold. We moved in winter. The removal director asked, "What on earth makes you move from Devon to Denton in January?"

I said, "It's with my work."

A reply came quickly: "Well, I don't think much about your boss. Who is he?"

Quite sheepishly and then with a bit more courage I said, "Well, God actually!"

He said, "It must be God to move you on this freezing cold January day to Lancashire."

We sat with our overcoats on, near to the meter. It was then a two-shilling meter and we were pouring the two-shillings into the meter just to keep ourselves warm. The church did have some problems in the sale of the house but their desire was that whoever came to lead the church would be given the option, when they settled, whether to stay in the church manse or to buy their own house. We took the second option which I am sure was the best one. After some time, the difficulties were overcome and the oversight offered us a loan of £3,000 as a deposit and I got the remainder of the money from my parents. The deposit was to be paid back by an arrangement which God enabled us to do. So we moved into 9 Shanklin Close in Haughton Green where we spent many happy years. We were very happy in that home. In fact, when we sold it, we had the benefit of the increase of house prices and were able, very quickly, to pay back the deposit to the church after everything was settled up.

So saying 'goodbye' to Exeter was a huge experience for us. Moving into unknown territory, coming from the south, words are different for everyday commodities. I was asking for 'baps' but now they were called 'ovenbottoms', 'balm cakes' and 'flour cakes'. We soon adapted but it was certainly colder and we missed the warm, milder weather of Devon. We were in the place were God had placed us, in a thriving church begun by Eddie Durham, and then E J Shearman pastored it for many years, followed by Ernest Anderson and then me. So I followed some excellent men. Ken Healey who assisted Ernest Anderson stayed for a little while and was a great help to me. Ken moved on to other work for the Lord.

Prior to us leaving Exeter for Denton, Sylvia had been working for the Danish Bacon Company and had a wonderful job in Exeter. But towards the end of our stay there, she had secured a job as a medical secretary, and she loved it, but in a matter of weeks the Lord called us to move to Denton in Greater Manchester. I didn't think there would be any chance of her having a similar job. However, when we moved into Haughton Green, Sylvia went down to the health centre to see if there was any chance of a job, even if it was only part-time or to fill in at holiday times. Unfortunately there were no jobs at that time, but one of the doctors took her telephone number, and soon after Sylvia received a call asking her if she would do some holiday relief work. Sylvia accepted and the holiday relief work turned into a full-time job. The doctor, Amy Montgomery, together with her husband, who was also a doctor, had practices in the same building. But their marriage was in difficulties. Doctor Amy asked Sylvia what it was about her that was different. Sylvia told her that she was a Christian and that her husband was a minister at the Pentecostal church.

"Praise God," she exclaimed, surprising Sylvia somewhat.

Sylvia asked, "Why do you say that?"

Amy responded, "Because I am a backslidden Pentecostal." In fact her father was the treasurer of the Burnley Assembly of God. She explained that she had wanted somebody to come into her life at this difficult stage and lead her back to Jesus. So they knelt down in the surgery and Doctor Amy gave her life to Christ. This story is quite sad as not long after that the marriage broke up and Doctor Brian died, although not before I had the opportunity of taking him to the Platt Fields recreation grounds in Manchester where an American evangelist was preaching and Doctor Brian gave his life to Jesus. By the end of the crusade he was giving out the songbooks. Tragically soon after the crusade he died in his middle 30s.

God is good, He does guide, and when one door closes another opens. Sylvia's employment in that surgery lasted many happy years before we left Denton and moved up to Bolton. It was a great change for the children, and I wonder whether we considered them enough when those moves were made. Sharon changed schools four times in one year, and this was not easy for her.

The church grew in Denton and we did extend the building and re-designed it in the October, and by the following Easter the church was full again. These were days of great conventions and great gatherings of God's people. So many were called to God's work and so many were filled with the Spirit and blessed in that building in Denton.

Our memories go back to some fantastic outpourings of God's Spirit upon those people. The Denton quartet was in full vogue when we moved there. In fact the first public meeting we went to, outside of the church, was in the Free Trade Hall in Manchester for a big national youth rally in which the Denton quartet were singing. They were quite renowned at the time; we had lots of qualified and talented people in the church. We began different ministries there which developed in many different ways.

One physical and natural problem that we had was that in the car park was a large mine shaft that was about twelve feet in diameter and about eight feet high above ground level. We were told it probably went down about 150 feet below the ground. It actually became what was advertised or publicised in the local newspaper as 'the largest dustbin in Denton'. People brought their huge pieces of furniture. How many pianos went down that shaft I don't know. We campaigned for it to be capped at ground level but were unsuccessful. The round wall had to be regularly checked for safety reasons and the barbed wire on top never lasted long before the next load of rubbish was disposed of down the shaft. It was a nuisance because it took the place of a number of spaces in our car park which we needed, plus it was quite dangerous.

The building was ideally situated in the town so we held many evangelistic outreaches. The new bypass was built which just passed the church. On the opening day we decided we would walk the length of it with an open-air witness and, praise God, that brought quite a stir in the town. One young boy saw us and decided that he would come to the evening Gospel meeting, and he gave his heart to Jesus. His name was Alan Molineaux who, with his wife, Beverley, went into God's work in Norfolk and pioneered into other villages. Alan got saved because we decided to walk the length of the motorway that day. Also from that church Steve and Joyce Dixon and Andy and Karen King have followed God's leading in their lives and gone into ministry around the world. Others followed like Bob and Joy Grahamslaw, now pastoring in Hadfield.

One year we planned a big tent crusade with Andrew Shearman the evangelist, and Ray Bevan the singer. Ray was little known outside of South Wales and this he described as his 'big break'. When he saw the number of young people in the tent he was wanting so much to preach as he felt that, with his testimony and background, he might be more relevant than Andrew. We did seek God for His guidance and they were able to share their ministry. We thank God that from then onwards Ray blossomed in his gifting and God has accomplished so much through him in Newport, Gwent and worldwide. Lancashire is an area of traditional marches and demonstrations. A couple of times a year we would march around Denton and witness for Jesus. We would get involved in carnivals and again we would witness for Jesus. We started many ventures such as the 'Tuesday Special', the senior citizens' meeting and caring for disabled people. We had an eye for all kinds of people.

It seemed that God had something to teach us a second time about saving money. With Sylvia working full-time we were beginning to save a little money for holidays etc, and decided this time to seek advice. We looked in the church magazine and saw an advertisement for a Christian company. The representative called and we duly signed up our small savings. Not long afterwards we read and heard of the Barlow Clowes collapse. We then found that our money was invested with that company and we lost out a second time. Some years later the Government were forced to intervene because the company was registered with the appropriate body. We eventually had a percentage returned to us but of course interest and some capital was lost. Lord what are you trying to say to us, is it not good to save? I wish I had the answer!

Then God laid upon my heart a great desire to reach out to the community, to people who were not coming into church. My wife and I thought we would start a telephone ministry and call it 'Lifeline Ministries'. We could not actually sell the plan to the church right in the beginning, so we decided to run and finance it ourselves. We began on our wedding anniversary on 15th June 1975. Every day we would put a fresh message on the telephone and people would ring in and receive it and leave any message they wanted, for any help or a visit. We were greatly helped because we could run this 24 hours a day, for we had two wonderful ladies in the church, Mrs Wilsea and Mrs Hickman, who were disabled and in wheelchairs. They were available right through the night. So we had somebody on call all the time. We had to be careful how we advertised this ministry. We did decide at one time that we would call it 'Phone a Friend'. We had some strange phone calls until we changed the name. I felt led of God to go to the London and Provincial Poster Company in Swinton. I went to see the managing director to ask if I could hire some space on large hoardings. I guessed that this would cost thousands of pounds, which we couldn't afford anyway. With great trepidation I went into his office, and he asked me what it was about. I told him it was free of charge, it was to help people and we had no hidden motive. He asked, "Well, how many hoardings do you want?"

I asked God to give me the words and said, "Well, hundreds rather than dozens." I didn't know what I was asking for but I do know that he responded: "Will 400 do?"

I said, "It depends on the cost."

He said, "I've not talked about cost at all." Four hundred posters for probably about ten years would have cost tens of thousands of pounds. Of course I knew what was happening. Rather than have no posters up on their hoardings between big contracts, the company would prefer to put something up. So when there was a lean time our posters would go up. They were not dated so it didn't matter.

Through that ministry, and through those wonderful women, many people were helped. People were helped to resist the seduction of suicide. People were healed over the telephone and saved. This caused quite a stir. So much so that the broadcasting people in Manchester got hold of it. Both the BBC and the big commercial radio station, Radio Piccadilly, were in touch for interviews. This gave us more publicity. In fact, while I was at Piccadilly Radio, I reminded them of a little knowledge I had gleaned, that by law they should have five minutes of religious broadcasting per week. That's religious broadcasting, not necessarily Christian. The managing director was not interested as it was not commercial. I said, "Sir, whether you are interested or not it is a law of the land."

He said, "Well, nobody else has asked me about it."

So I said, "Well, I am!"

Eventually, by my persistence, he said, "Well, are you interested in doing it?" This was just what I wanted to hear!

"OK," he said. "Five minutes per night, probably between midnight and four o'clock in the morning, when the least number of people are listening." But then the least number of people that ever listened to Piccadilly between that particular hour was 12,000. I reckon that was a pretty good congregation! He said, "No mentioning 'Jesus', no 'Bible-thumping'.

I said, "That's fine."

I remember going to a District Council meeting, telling the pastors about it and asking them to pray. One pastor got up and said, "You're wasting your time, Terry! If you can't preach heaven and hell and so forth, you are wasting your time."

I said, "No! I am going to build bridges." And that's what I did. I started off with just a little moral story and eventually I was able to talk about Jesus, about the cross, about being born-again, etc. For 140 consecutive nights, God gave me that opportunity.

Soon I was asked to visit all the Regional Councils of the British Assemblies of God. This I did in the next twelve months, covering each one. Brethren were kind as I shared my vision. So many thought I was doing this as a means of preparing for the General Council Appointment of Broadcasting Director. I did not feel I had the technical ability to contemplate such a task; what I could do was inspire, help to raise money and be a useful member of the team. For over twelve years I was Chairman and, more my forte, the radio evangelist. Sylvia also presented programmes for some time in the Rimini area and our son, Jason, who was just a teenager, helped with news items for British holiday makers. This with carefully chosen music and the clear presentation proved most rewarding. Two men visiting Italy on business from the

UK contacted the local Italian office after hearing Sylvia's programme. They were given the help they required and were directed to the nearest Assembly of God when back in the UK and subsequently became born-again believers.

When we went to Rome we broadcast to the English people while they were on holiday during the summer period. Wonderful letters came to us eventually about what God had done through the radio. Contacts in Italy and the UK were passed to the relevant pastors. Not only that, the BBC invited us at Denton, to have a morning service on national radio. This was a great opportunity to broadcast the Gospel to around a million people, we were told by the BBC producer. He said that the programme was excellently received by the listeners, and he requested a similar programme to be recorded for broadcast the following Sunday over the BBC World Service, with a possible 38 million people listening. We did it and had a wonderful time. Jim Bowler gave a testimony, Daphne Kynaston sang 'People Need the Lord', and I presented the programme and preached the Gospel. It was a thrilling service.

Letters received

I was so delighted to receive a letter from a former Baptist minister by the name of Rev Francis Dixon, from Bournemouth, who was a regular broadcaster and well known throughout the country, complimenting us on the programme:

> *"I sat in my car by the sea and rejoiced with you all and prayed with you for the many who were listening."*

This is typical of the scores of letters that arrived from all over the world following the morning service from Carmel Pentecostal Church, Denton on Radio 4 on September 28th 1980.

> Another letter from a Jesuit priest in Amsterdam:
> *"You talk about Jesus but the Jesus you know is different to the Jesus I know. Please tell me more about Him."*

From Richmond, Surrey:
"Thank you so much for your letter. I feel that God is somehow listening to you and in a way, to me. I was at my wits' end when I turned to your programme. Asking you to pray for me seemed forward of me. I feel I am no longer alone. The hearing in my right ear is back to normal. I can hear the birds outside."

From Edinburgh:
"When I first wrote asking for prayer, I could not walk except with sticks. This has been the case for many years. Then I began to feel that I was moving easier and my movements were freer. Then I found I could move around without my sticks and I put it down to my faith in the Lord Jesus and your prayers."

From Kent:
Although the lady that we requested prayer for suffering from cancer has died, we read the Scriptures you gave to us for her. She found peace with her Saviour just hours before she died."

From Leeds:
"I don't often listen to the radio, but I did that morning. How grateful I am, for now I have found hope again in the Saviour."

One family had recently returned to Britain from New Zealand after searching for satisfaction. The husband tuned to the radio and heard the service. He looked in the telephone directory to see if there was an Assembly of God nearby. He found a telephone number, enquired about the evening service, got in his car, went to the Gospel service and was wonderfully saved.

Cries for spiritual help and prayer come in dozens of letters. Doctors, university lecturers, surgeons, music teachers and well-known authors have been among the enquirers. A Jesuit priest who had studied at Harvard and Yale universities wanted to know more about the living Saviour. All praise to the Lord!

One letter was received from Kampala University hospital in Uganda. The man was so broken in spirit that he didn't know which way to turn. He was a famous gynaecologist who had never lost a baby at birth. He was there at the birth of his own child, the child lived but he lost his wife. Just at the moment when I was saying, "Your life is in pieces and you do not know which way to turn," he turned his radio on in his office in Kampala and heard the words, "It is like a jigsaw puzzle with pieces not fitting in so well." He turned to Christ. He wrote to me and told me the story and gave his life back to Christ. From South America, from Australia, from Asia, letters were coming because the BBC had allowed me to advertise an address, which people had said that they would never allow me to do. They said that they had never been asked. The post office people were so accommodating. They said, "We will make sure that all your mail comes direct to your house." It was a simple address: Lifeline, Denton, Manchester, UK, and it came direct to me. Hundreds of letters were coming to me every day. God was so good because now I was asked to broadcast around the world on different stations. Wonderful things happened through that. We built a studio at Denton in part of the building and there we started broadcasting from the Isle of Man's Radio Manx. It was £15 for 15 minutes. We started in that simple way until, eventually, I was broadcasting to China and India and most of the continents of the world. From that little studio we produced a program that was sent out to Trans World Radio, Far Eastern Broadcasting Council and other stations, and we got a wonderful team together. David Carr was a tremendous help. He was a man of all trades and had a great big heart and helped me so much, as did David Wadsworth, Barbara Hilton, Lily Fletcher and others. Sylvia got involved. She was the first lady to present programmes for the Assemblies of God Broadcasting Council.

So that began my passion to reach as many for Jesus as possible and by all means. '**People need the Lord**' has been my driving force. Eventually I became chairman of the Assemblies of God Broadcasting Council.

Broadcasting Council

After serving many years on the Council, travelling to many parts of the world and taking seminars, I knew God's promise was being fulfilled in my life. I had never been taught broadcasting skills, and had never been in a college for media studies, but through observation of my mentors and God's calling on my life I took the opportunity He gave me. I wish I had been taught more of the technical side. God can take the 'nobodies' and make them into what He desires. God can take those who feel they have nothing, but if you are sold out to God, He can make something of your life.

For many years we continued our Lifeline telephone ministry with around a quarter of a million calls to the telephone service each year. Then we developed a cassette ministry, sending ministry cassettes around the world, and then God opened other doors of service for Him.

CHAPTER SEVEN

In journeyings oft (2 Cor. 11:26)

One of the great joys and privileges that we have had is to visit Israel and the surrounding countries many times. I first visited Israel through the kindness of a man named Harold Watson while in the early days of my ministry in Exeter. He had been to Israel and told me that he wanted to send me to Israel to benefit my ministry rather than wait until the end of my life. So off we went to Israel for £108. I persuaded my Aunt Eunice and father-in-law to come with me and we had a terrific time. After that I took tours to Israel about a dozen times. I had the joy of helping people to visit that land who would not have been able to go otherwise, and that included my wife, children and my Uncle Alwyn. It was my uncle's greatest joy and the highlight of his life to visit the land that he would never have been able to visit without my help. Many outstanding events took place on those tours. We had unsaved and unchurched people with us and invariably, to God be the glory, many came to know Christ. In fact, outstanding memories include baptising new converts in the Jordan River and seeing them going on with God and being established in churches back in this country. Many things happened which were quite extraordinary. On one occasion, Mrs Watson, the mother of Ian Watson, pastor at Bolton, was crossing the Sea of Galilee, when suddenly she noticed that her handbag had rolled off the side of the boat. We didn't know how far back it had gone overboard. I went to the captain and asked if there was any possibility of turning the boat around. He said it was impossible as he did not know how far we had gone since missing the valuables. "Look at the waves!" he said. It was a boisterous day, it would be quite impossible to locate this bag but in the bag was all that Mrs Watson owned: her passports, her money, her tickets, everything that was precious to her. After a lot of persuasion, the captain turned the boat around. There were about a hundred people on the boat so it was quite a large boat.

He retraced the way he came and said, "It is just impossible on this vast lake. How on earth are we going to find a bag?" Those who had binoculars were scouring the sea and eventually someone saw something bobbing up on the water. Fortunate or God's goodness? The handbag had been placed and tied in a polythene bag that had made it float on the water. When we got nearer, one of the crew dived in and recovered the bag, which took great courage. That was to us quite a miracle. We were praying and believing that God would help us. We took a collection and I think the captain was quite happy when we gave him what we had given out of our love and appreciation. God was so good.

On some of our earlier trips we were able to visit places that you can't go to now, like Hebron and Samaria. We had some wonderful experiences in Samaria near the well where Jesus met the outcast. We learned a lot about the Samaritan people. There are still about 200 living reclusively outside the city. These would be original Samaritans. It was a great opportunity to talk to both Jews and Samaritans as we mixed now whereas 2,000 years ago it was quite unknown. We were able to share Jesus Christ in little house meetings in Jerusalem and with those whom we had known from past years by name, John Foster and his wife, for example, at the International Christian Embassy. We also met up with other Christians and shared our testimonies with joy. Our group also met in the hotel in the morning, and during night meetings we would get to know those who were not walking with the Lord. At those times, great counselling would go on until the early hours and we would have to be up around 5am next morning for our trips.

The days were so hot that we had to do as much as we could during the early part of the day. We had precious times when we broke bread and had communion on the lakeside where Jesus had His encounters with His disciples. We had great moments on the Mount of Olives when we read the Scriptures about the coming of Christ to somewhere in that area of the mountain. It was quite interesting, for on one occasion a tour leader said, "Of course, I get to know the (tour) groups. If the group is mainly Roman Catholics they will be asking, 'Where is the exact spot where Jesus ascended to heaven?'" Concrete footprints were put there recently to satisfy some. And many naively believe that they are the footprints of Jesus. When it came to evangelicals, to say that it happened "somewhere in this area" was enough to satisfy them. But to look up to the sky and know that Jesus ascended and will descend to that spot was of great inspiration. We had tremendous times when we broke bread in the garden of Gethsemane and the garden of Gordon's Calvary, not inside the Church of the Holy Sepulchre but out among the groves and fig trees, the almond blossoms and the tranquil atmosphere in that place, called the Place of the Skull. There, too, many encounters with Christ and deeper commitments were made. We did have bad experiences too, when money, bags and even passports were stolen. The real nuisance of children begging – they were almost professional beggars at the young age of eight or nine and younger – who would mingle among you, almost walking between your legs and trying to divide you and get bags from you. One of the sad things was, and I learnt this from going to India, that in India if you gave them a penny it was so precious, but if you gave coins to the beggars in Jerusalem they would throw them on the ground in disgust as they wanted notes and bigger amounts. Real poverty I have never seen outside of India, but Israel is the place where probably the most moving, deep spiritual experiences were ours. The joy was ours to go to Jordan and visit Petra and take a trip down through the very narrow rock entrance into the 'Pink City', the 'Glowing City of Petra'. My wife was last in the row. We had to go on horses and she did not like them. We could not always keep together. One boy took a liking to my wife and especially to her cap. He eventually got her cap, which she regretted afterwards because it had sheltered her from the sun, and she was never able to find another like the one that she had given away. These were experiences that we will never forget. We had the opportunity to go into Jordan near the border of Sudan, down to Egypt and visit the Nile River. Here again there are pockets of Christians who are meeting together at the risk of their lives and we need to pray for them in these lands because they are finding faith in the Lord Jesus Christ.

It has been my great privilege to travel many parts of the world, nearly 70 countries and the majority of the continents. The joy has been not only to learn about the culture and the ways of people, and the relative value of money but, even more importantly, to preach the Gospel of Jesus Christ and to teach and commission young men into the ministry.

Travelling around the world preaching in the main cities of Australia we eventually arrived in the Barrier Reef area. What a joy to meet Tony Hallo in Townsville. Tony is a great man of God and he gave me many wonderful opportunities for ministry. On our way to Australia we stopped for some days in Singapore and ministered there in their fine churches, and we were wonderfully cared for by Pastor Pang and also in Hong Kong with Pastor Ip. Again we experienced so much friendship and joy in seeing great fruitfulness through our ministry. The benefit of travelling and seeing other cultures and forms of ministry are that friendships are formed and one's vision is expanded and we are challenged more for mission. Of recent times I have gone to very poor countries. I have said, "Lord, I want to go where the need is, and where the need is that is the call."

Together with me has been my faithful and zealous wife, Sylvia. She too has been blessed of God. She has spoken at the General Conference and led meetings there. God has used her in counselling to a great extent. The quiet one in the background who takes every opportunity for Jesus. Much is being done with a particular missions emphasis. Not great numbers but great results. I want to say that whatever you are available for, God will see that He uses you. Don't seek the great until you are faithful in the small. Have a big dream and a big vision but hold things to yourself.

Even on our silver wedding anniversary I found myself preaching in Nassau in the Bahamas and Montego Bay, Jamaica, where people were gloriously saved. I had a scare here in the local Assembly of God for I was preaching in the church with no air conditioning with a temperature of 120°F inside and higher outside. When I visited the bathroom I was passing blood and I was rushed to my hotel room and ordered to stay in a dark room for 48 hours. However when I was restored I enjoyed the world's best milk shakes but did not like the huge jelly fish covering the sands where we were staying.

Preaching in Sweden and Norway and some parts of Russia was different. Yet one of my most satisfying visits was to Bairlini prison in Glasgow where, after sharing the Gospel, a number of men stayed behind to accept Christ as Saviour.

Southern Ireland

During my pastorate in Denton, the church leaders asked if I would like to visit Ireland, flying into Cork in the south and returning from Belfast in the north. I had a great burden for Ireland. There were a few contacts, mainly telephone numbers. I rang them and asked God to guide me where we could, in the future, help and support. I landed in Cork and had a very interesting time. I stayed in quite spartan accommodation. I saw life as it would have been, possibly 50 years ago. I lived on spam and 'tatties', and a big shaggy dog had to be kicked off the mattress, which was directly on the floor, so that the pastor could have his bed for the night. From there I travelled up to Limerick. I did not meet many folk there, but when I revisited that area some years later I saw some small churches that God was helping with good leadership; this was a great encouragement. I moved on to the border town of Dundalk, one of the main IRA towns just over the border from the north. One man met me on that cold, damp, miserable morning on the rail station platform at Dundalk: his name was Wilf O'Brennan; I had never met him before. Wilf was born in Dundalk, and had been a bank manager. He had retired and with his wife, Joan, went to Mattersey Bible College to work. Joan was the cook there for many years. Then God called them back to their home town of Dundalk to pioneer a work for Him in one of the hardest places I have ever been. Holding open-air meetings in the centre of Dundalk was not easy, but we were right next to the street market stalls. Owners and customers alike had to hear the Gospel. One young stall holder who also had shops at Blackrock was very interested in the message we preached and this resulted in a long-time friendship. Last year after a break of around twelve years, I visited Danny, who remembered those days and the message we preached. It was just Wilf, Joan and myself at times, standing in the open air, preaching the Gospel in this antagonistic, deeply Roman Catholic community that did not want anyone invading the town; the political strife and atmosphere could almost be cut with a knife. There were bullet marks behind us on the town hall buildings. We took our lives in our hands, but God was with us.

The harvest we saw in that IRA border town was tremendous. People responded to the Gospel in every meeting in the makeshift 'hall', which was Wilf's garage with benches around the perimeter. Once recognising their acceptance of Jesus as Lord, folk were invited into the living room where repentance and discipleship took place. Many had great opposition from their Catholic families and workmates, some losing their jobs – the Catholic priests who had great power and influence would see to that. But God kept them and a number entered the work of the Lord. One young Catholic woman who was a ward sister in the local hospital was forced out of her position for leaving 'The Church', but soon she went out as a missionary to Africa.

One of Wilf's friends from Five Mile Hill just over the border at Newry always supported the meetings. He was a farmer with a very deep but quiet voice, but with a great love for the Lord. There was a long driveway up to his farmhouse. He built a house for the Lord at the entrance to the drive. His aged mother played an old pedal-organ; chickens were still in the hall and sometimes ran around between our legs. Later, he built a very fine church on the opposite side of the driveway. The enemy gave him a hard time and many attempts were made to drive the family away from the area. He stocked car and lorry tyres and eventually someone set fire to the business and he lost all his assets, but lives were spared. I was honoured to be a guest at the farmhouse many times. They were people who knew God and who supported God's work and his servants.

In fact we felt that we should follow this up with a crusade one summer and the young people's group from our church in Denton went over to Dundalk by minibus. We toured the streets and advertised the meetings, which were held in the town hall. On the first night, no one turned up at all. What should we do? Ian Watson was in charge of the group and they were a fine committed group of young people. I was so disappointed for them. I said, "We will conduct services at half seven as advertised." No congregation, that was extremely difficult. I said, "We will do it, we will pray and we will conduct the service because we have advertised it, although there is no one here." Towards the end of the service, one man struggled into the building. He was drunk. Wilf kept him up for some hours, sobering him up with strong coffee, and eventually told him about Jesus. We persisted, we prayed, we worked, we advertised, and by the end of the week there were about 40 people in that town hall. We had the joy of seeing many of them surrender to Jesus Christ. That started a tremendous friendship between Joan, Wilf and myself. They lived at Blackrock, just a mile out from the centre of Dundalk, overlooking the sea, a beautiful spot, in a little Irish cottage. Wilf even baptised there, he would study the tides and dig a hole at the appropriate time, waiting for the sea to come in and fill it, and then the baptismal service would be timed so that there was enough water in the hole to baptise them.

That first visit to Ireland I shall never forget because I was bitterly cold. I had not taken adequate clothing with me. I walked around with my pyjamas underneath my top clothes, they were the only extra warmth that I had. But there was a beautiful hot bath waiting for me in Wilf's home. Joan had made a sumptuous tea for she was a fantastic cook. I shall never forget the warm welcome of these two intrepid pioneer warriors working for God in this town. My heart was akin to them. For many years I travelled back and forth to Dundalk. I have mentioned the difficult circumstances: buildings, warmth, attractiveness. There were not many advantages, but there was the love of Jesus, and many of those who came to Jesus have gone on to serve God in leadership both in Ireland and in other parts of the world. I am so glad to have had a part in that wonderful missionary endeavour, pioneering a work in Dundalk. The wonderful building is now a testimony to the sacrifice of Joan and Wilf. Tragically Wilf had a stroke early one morning and was found slumped over the stones outside the building. He did however last long enough to be wheeled into the church on the day on which it was opened, when my cousin Aeron Morgan from Australia and I were the guest preachers. Wilf went to be with the Lord in heaven, having run his race and accomplished the task, but the work of God continues.

I always gave my mum and dad a report of where I was and what I was doing. In fact I would write a letter every Monday. On this occasion I wrote from Dundalk. Dad always wrote back and although not yet a Christian the stock phrase was "glad to hear of good results". Remember, he was a footballer. He wrote to tell me that he knew Dundalk, it was the last football match he ever played in after moving from Wolverhampton Wanderers to Ireland. It was customary that the visiting team to Dundalk were thrown in the river after the match. That river runs behind the new Assembly. His son preaching where his dad years before played soccer. In perhaps a strange way he was proud of me.

One time, when we were in Bantry Bay, we could only hire a narrow room in a public house, about twelve foot by 30 foot, between two bars. We sang 'Since Jesus Came Into My Heart' until drinkers, having to feed their inquisitiveness, opened the doors either side. What they saw rather bemused them, seeing us enjoying ourselves. We had the joy of explaining ourselves afterwards to some, for after all we were drinking of the water that never shall cause thirst again! Some of those attending this meeting had walked miles over mountains to get there. Bus services are not frequent in those parts of the south. The joy of seeing people come to faith in Christ compensated adequately for the effort made by the folk from Bantry. Miraculously some got saved that night. Pastor David Lowe, apart from being a full-time farmer, looks after God's sheep. It was with great joy that I heard of the opening of the new building in Bantry Bay in 2004.

Northern Ireland – Belfast

Sylvia came with me on one trip to Belfast, where we experienced God's protection yet again. We were on our way home for lunch when we realised we had forgotten to buy our son a present, as we were leaving for the UK the next day. We retraced our steps to a sports shop to buy some socks. While we were in the shop we heard gun fire outside; news came to us later that Gerry Adams, a leading IRA member, was walking the same route we had just taken and a sniper in a passing car attempted to shoot Mr Adams. God had preserved us again.

My first visit to Belfast was in the midst of the fighting. I walked through houses abandoned on the Shankhill Road. It was eerie for everything had been taken out so there could be no looting. An emergency call arrived at Pastor Harry Letson's house. Huge fires were burning in the area of his church. Military and police vehicles circled the area. People had set alight their own homes so that others could not use them. The Assembly was right in the centre of the blazes. Harry was allowed through a narrow walkway to see if anything could be rescued. He opened the church doors and there wasn't even a sniff of smoke. Praise God for His protection. Bethshan at the city end of the Shankhill was safe and prospering, as also were the other Assemblies.

My first visit to Letterkenny in the north-west corner of Ireland was a visit I shall not forget. Pastor Mike McBride and his wife have done a marvellous work for God. What meetings. What outpourings. What hungry people. A visit to the home of a severely sick brother blessed me so much. I was in the area for a convention and this brother depended on radio for his Christian input – he was completely bedfast. We prayed and praised.

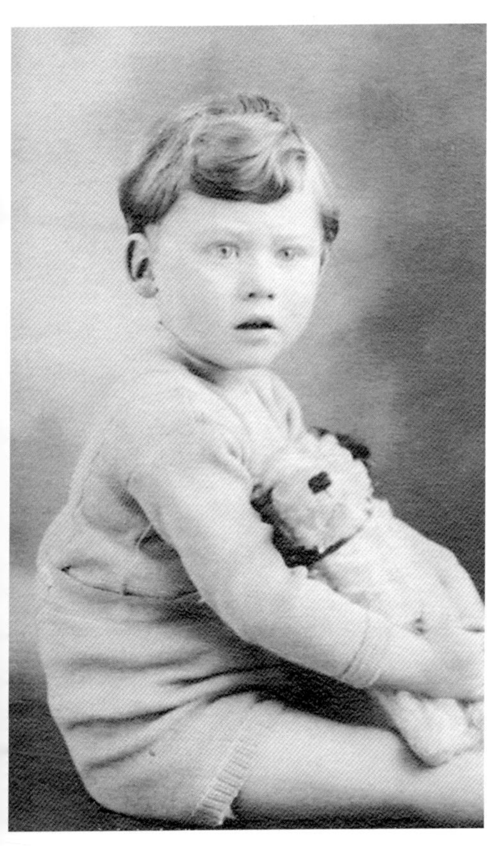

This is me in 1938, aged two.
I was born as 'Colin',
but my parents quickly
renamed me 'Terence'

My grandmother,
Mrs Elizabeth Lewis

Uncle Alwyn *(far left)* and my mum with Aunt Eunice. I had no brothers or sisters, and Alwyn and Eunice adopted me as their 'little brother'

Above: My mum and dad
Left: Sylvia and me
Below: Sylvia's parents, Pastor Harry and Daisy Weare

The AoG Youth Choir in Aberaman, during my early years in my home church

Clockwise from above:
Howard Carter;
Lester Sumrall;
Leonard Ravenhill;
George Stormont;

Centre: Tommy Evans,
who baptised me
in water

Sylvia and I on our wedding day on 15th June, 1957, at Crosskeys AoG

With Sylvia at our first church in Peterborough, 1957

At our church in Peterborough with the deacon, Mr Porter *(left)*, and one of the elders, Mr Ware *(far right)*

Children from Peterborough saved money to help support missionaries

Speaking at the Assemblies of God General Conference in 1986

Left: Learning to fly!

Below: A Walk of Witness held in Denton, where we pastored our fourth church

I once preached at a graduation ceremony at the Southern Cross Bible College in Australia. This was the first time I had ever worn a gown, and the Australian heat was sweltering. With me are Bryn Barratt *(centre)* and my cousin, Aeron Morgan, Principal of the Bible college.

With Laurence Hennesey of Breakfree Ministries, Bolton. Laurence and his wife, Iris, ran 'The Haven' rehabilitation centre near Dublin before they moved back to Bolton.

Left:
Pastor Keating and his wife and family, from Waterford, Eire, where I preached many times

Below:
In 2002 I spent time reaching out to street people from Lower East Side in New York

Beside the Volga River. Jim and Margaret Preece introduced me to Russia;
Left to right: Emma Worthington; Maureen Molajo; Jim; Margaret; and me

Left:
Preaching during a baptism in Samara, Russia, which included one of our team, Maureen Molajo. Pastor Oleg *(second left)* hosted the meeting

Right:
My friend Cyril Cartwright and I joined the 'March For Jesus' in Minsk, Belarus; Cyril is now the treasurer of Lifeline Ministries

In Russia, I took in the historical sights of Moscow, including the Lenin Mausoleum in Red Square

Above:
Sylvia and I have had a toilet block dedicated to us after we donated money to a church in Russia. People travel from miles around to see the toilets!

Left:
These four young men walked from Burma (Myanmar) to a meeting for leaders in India; it was a dangerous two-week journey

Above:
Every member of this leper colony in South India is a Christian

Above:
As we left the leper colony, we saw an Indian couple worshipping the 'snake' god

Above:
Pastor P Prakasam with his wife and sister

Above: I visited lepers in their own church. This photo was taken outside the leper colony in South India

Above:
Evangelist Barry Woodward and I visited a widows' home in Coimbatore, South India. The women attend prayer group for eight hours a day

Right:
Job Prakasam, the first convert in his area, anointing me as bishop!

Right:
A group from our church leaders' conference in Malawi

Left:
Muslims coming to Christ in Malawi

Left:
With Steve Mbwana *(left)* and Dr Lazarus Chakawara, Principal of the AoG Bible College in Malawi

Some of the 17 bicycles bought for evangelists trained to reach into villages. Every week an average of 50 people are converted through each evangelist's ministry.

Right:
My wife Sylvia was the first female Assemblies of God presenter to broadcast on radio

Above:
Peter Yates *(left)*, my closest friend and sponsor

Below:
Broadcasting to Bolton from the Claremont Chapel studio: *(back row, from left)* Ian Watson, pastor of Bolton Pentecostal Church; me; Mike Shaft of Piccadilly Radio; *(front)* the Mayor and Mayoress of Bolton

Left:
A reunion of former Denton pastors in 2003

Right:
A building bought from Manchester City Mission to pioneer a church in Hyde, Cheshire; the place was ancient and uninviting, but it was ours!

Below: The original church building of Assemblies of God in Hyde, which has now been bought back by local members after 70 years as a non-Pentecostal church

Right:
Sylvia and I with our daughter, Sharon, and son, Jason

Left:
Standing on the top step with me is my mother, Aunt Eunice and Lily Fletcher from Hyde; behind us is our son, Jason; our daughter, Sharon *(front left)*, is holding her son – my grandson – Scott; and Lauren, my grandaughter, is next to Sylvia *(front right)*

Right:
Sylvia and I with my cousins, Aeron and Peter Morgan, and their wives, in Australia

Above:
Jason's children, Jack and Scarlet, were my first grandchildren; Jack became famous as the young lad featured in TV adverts for Safeway supermarkets

Above:
I have no brothers or sisters, but Sylvia has one sister, Margaret Miles. Margaret and her husband, Maurice, served in the early days of the Congo Evangelistic Mission

Right:
My parents celebrating Mum's 80th birthday

Left:
Our sapphire wedding anniversary – celebrating 45 years together

Today, I remain determined to go to heaven with my boots on. My present 'retirement' includes directing Lifeline Ministries and broadcasting as a radio preacher to Africa.

The countryside was magnificent; Irish hospitality is the best. I have always been impressed by the standard of commitment, deportment and dress of the young people. I am happy to say that what I've seen and heard from the Cork area is so encouraging. Men with big hearts and big vision seeing hundreds in their meetings, whereas a few years ago there were only a few meeting in the pastor's lounge. Men like Nick Cassidy are pioneering in the 'red-light' district of Cork, hiring halls at astronomical rates. The faithfulness of Tony and Agneta Simpson has astounded me, and now other men are finding a 'new breath of God' on the land.

What about America?

The land flowing with milk and honey. The streets are paved with gold. On the first two occasions I was invited to the States, I was abandoned in New York. On the first occasion I had very little money so I had to go to an old doss-house and hire the top room in the house for three dollars. I could not afford their breakfast, not that I particularly wanted it, but I had a drink at the side of the road, a piece of toast and a drop of orange juice for 50 cents. It is a long story, but I was there at the invitation of the conference secretary as a gift of appreciation for what I did in organising the World Conference for the Full Gospel Businessmen's Fellowship. Communications have since broken down, so I shall never go to America again. I had no need to go but I was invited some years later by a pastor from my own home assembly in South Wales. I felt I could trust him. I arrived in Oakland where his wife met me.

I said, "Where is your husband?"

She said, "He is in another part of the country, but we have arranged for you to go up to Medland, a little town in Oregon."

I landed in Medland by Greyhound Coach and found that the man I was to stay with was almost destitute. He was pioneering a church, but didn't have a building, so he hired a school where he lived with his family. A school room was quickly adapted into a bedroom, where I stayed for a week. We went down into the town, rolled a few handbills off the printer and gave them out. It was the time of the charismatic movement. Some people came into the meetings, but our salvation was that one man came and gave to the pastor and to me a hundred dollar bill which just about paid for the food while I was there. I had already used the money I had brought to provide for our needs. I came home and said, "Never again!" Maybe it is dangerous to say "Never again."

My friend George Stormont, who was at one time pastor at Bethshan Tabernacle, Manchester, went to Duluth in Minnesota to pastor toward the end of his ministry. George invited me to go to Duluth to preach at their Annual Convention. I had a terrific time – things were so different this time.

When the members asked, "But where are your wife and children?" I said, "Well, they are at home as it is too expensive for us all to come." The next year tickets came for all of us. We went to the convention and preached there. They had arranged a trip down to Disney Land in Florida for Jason, Sharon, Sylvia and me; how God had rewarded and blessed us.

I went back to the States a number of times preaching, especially with my dear friend Roger Blackmore, there in Coram in New York State. How good that church was. Just in recent times Roger telephoned us and invited us to go for some ministry and dedicate his grandchild, and they would add on a week's holiday, completely free of charge, in Pennsylvania. What a joy! Yes, Paul said he learnt to be without and rejoiced in it and when he had much he rejoiced as well. God has been good to us. On my last visit I had the unforgettable experience of preaching and feeding the street people in the Lower East side of New York City, ending at about 2am in the 'Paradise Hotel' where the simple call: "Food! Come and get it!" brought down-and-outs in various stages of undress hurrying to get the hot meal prepared for them. Roger was Chairman of the Hope Foundation charity, but it was run by Dianne Dunne, a woman of great vision, and a small team of helpers.

We always have to be wise and follow God's leading. One time, when I went to the States and landed in New York, I wanted to meet with David Wilkinson and Leonard Ravenhill, in Brooklyn. I went on the Metro, had my camera over my shoulder and my cases in my hand, and walked from street to street until I found the address from a road map. When I got to the door, Dave and Len said, "You didn't walk through the streets like that did you? You could have had a knife in your back for your camera! It is just amazing you have not been mugged." Ignorance is bliss. I was only in my 20s then. I've encountered many dangerous experiences since.

Missionary visits

God gave me a great big missionary heart, so it was a tremendous challenge when I moved to Bolton, and Jim Preece, who was the chairman of the Full Gospel Businessmen's Fellowship in Bolton, asked me if I would like to go with him and his wife to Samara in Russia. We had to raise our own fare as we always do on these missions and God enabled me to do that with help from time to time from our church. On one mission per year they would cover the cost of transport and accommodation, which was a tremendous help. We always wanted to go with money to give to the work, to enhance the work, to encourage the workers. The liberal giving of God's people never failed.

We went to Samara. We were shocked when we got there and yet challenged because Oleg, the leader, and his wife were living on the premises while building this house for God. The upstairs was not completed – it was going to be a Sunday school and youth room – but the money had run out. We had sufficient money to give to them to complete that job. What a joy it was to feel that the House of God was erected in that former Communist country, and in that place people would come to know the Lord Jesus as their personal Lord and Saviour. That was a great trip. We travelled near and far to many churches, and had a wonderfully fruitful time – and lasting friendships began. We went across the Volga River to see a great site that was being earmarked for a youth camp and also for a rehabilitation centre for drug addicts and alcoholics. The pavements were full of such people; children and babies were discarded, too, in scenes that would break your heart. Russia is crying out now for the message of hope that it had rejected.

It was a privilege to have the freedom to hold open-air services on the street corners and in the squares, and publicly invite people to Christ with PA systems blaring out. We saw old women coming and kneeling, bare kneed, on cobbled ground at the feet of statues of Lenin and finding Jesus Christ as Lord and Saviour. Laws were passed not so long afterwards, forbidding house-groups. But just before that we went into homes, holding short times of fellowship, neighbours being invited in, maybe eight to ten people in the living room having a cup of tea and a piece of cake and then being exposed to the Gospel and responding. I have never seen such warm-hearted responses as I saw in Russia.

During our mission in Samara, on the first Sunday morning a man about 65 years of age came out for prayer. We had no idea of his need, as he spoke to us in Russian, but we prayed for him in spite of this. At the end of the mission this man came to the meeting and asked the pastor if he could give his testimony. This was in the form of a poem, but we had no idea what he was going to say. However, he told us through an interpreter that God had instantaneously delivered him from smoking after 50 years. He had not smoked from the time we prayed for him, which was over two weeks previously. Below is the interpretation of the poem he read in that meeting:

What am I living for?
Life is full of joy and tears,
And we often want to know the
Answer to the main question.

This question is in my mind,
Very often: What am I living for?
What for did my creator
Save my life so many times?
I was sick so many times.

I suffered much, and sometimes
Nearly lost my mind but
I have not lost my faith and love.

But I tried to get rid
Of my bad habits all by myself.
With my strength
I was searching for the truth,
Arguing with other people.

"Terry, you helped to open my spiritual eyes, to see Jesus as my Saviour, and I know you as my brother in the faith; you are so blessed by God, and you are the witness of God's love. The Holy Spirit came into my heart and I realised how wonderful is everything created by God. He is a God of miracles and we can see His love everywhere. I am weak but in Him I have strength. I have looked over all my life again and I have comprehended deeper what I am living for. I am living to fulfil His purpose on the earth and to bring God's Word to people showing His love and kindness."

This brother, whose name is Vasily, testified that he had given up smoking, which he started as a young boy in school. The pastor says God delivered him from this bad habit completely and he is now so happy. In subsequent years we have gone to the Ukraine and Belarus a number of times. The same kind of things have happened. In Belarus we have adopted a system of twinning churches, to find a church in the UK that would build ministry links of fellowship with a church in one of the Russian countries: communicating by email, getting to know each other and each other's church, pastor, leader and people. If possible the church in the UK would contribute the very small amount of £15 a month to support the pastor full-time. Small money but it goes a long way in those countries. We have succeeded in twinning up a small number of churches and could really do with more. You can't advertise meetings in these countries now, except by word of mouth. You cannot hire halls for the preaching of the Gospel. There are great difficulties, but people are coming to know Jesus. One church we returned to this past year we saw had doubled in numbers since the previous year – a year when we were very moved concerning the lack of facilities. They were short of toilets and we were told that they could put up a toilet block for $250, about £180. What a bargain! We did it and now it is a showpiece. People are travelling to see the block of toilets in the grounds of this church, and some are coming into the church and wanting to know more about Jesus.

What kind of church is it? Well, it is an old property, an old house that has been bricked around and, when completed, the old house was pulled down and the outer shell used for the Gospel. There were probably over 60 people crammed into that room and we were told that there were just as many as that who could not come. They have great need of transport. Some of the people live miles out, but they are prepared to walk. However some of them are now too old to walk distances. A minibus would be a tremendous help for churches like that. Many of these fellowships are out in forests. This is the way they pioneer: they don't go north, south, east or west, they start somewhere and then go to the next village and then the next. That is the way they successfully grow.

In one village there are 276 people living in total; 235 of them are saved. They built a magnificent building with their own hands over a long period of time. As money came in, so they would buy the necessary wood, windows, doors and concrete and eventually they completed that building.

There are amazing stories of God's visitation – God visiting young people during the time of communism and war, many of them being filled with the Holy Spirit. One little boy went to his unsaved father and told him that God gave him a dream that one day his father would be a pastor – he was not saved then. His father did become a pastor, a shepherd of God's flock. One young man, because he was a Christian, was taken to Siberia and dropped from a helicopter into the forests of Siberia to die. Miraculously, God provided one of his own creation, a bear, yes, a grizzly bear, to look after him, to warm him by night, to look after him during the day. This bear would go and collect berries and bring the berries to this young man. Eventually, he led him to a little crofter's cottage where he came back into normal life again. Amazing stories, God's outpouring in visions, prophecies to young people and teenagers. God has blessed even in the midst of infirmities, sicknesses, deprivation, poverty, famine of immense kind, but those people rejoice in the Lord. It has been our privilege to return to those countries and see what God is doing. From little, much can be done.

We find young men, who are now great interpreters, taking jobs to support themselves while they go on these missions and to help others to come to their country to preach the Gospel.

In 2003 we had the privilege of going down to Homel in the Chernobyl area where that great radiation leak occured in 1986, when thousands died and thousands were maimed. Very few foreign preachers have gone down to that area which is just on the border of Belarus and the Ukraine. They begged me to go and minister, and I said that Cyril, my travelling companion, and I would go, and trust God, which we did. We had tremendous meetings and great fellowship there – people so hungry for the Word. Although this was a midweek meeting, the building was full. In other countries churches are full whatever day you worship. In Homel a great work is being done by Pastor Serjay. His vision is to build a church of 300 people – that would be the maximum – and then he reaches out and plants another church. In ten years, he has planted 20 churches. He has almost 300 people now, extending the building sufficiently to hold the 300, then he is going to break out into more areas and see God move.

Men are volunteering to go forward, trusting God and with no financial backing to lead these pioneer churches. We want to do something for them, to help them reach that great country before it is too late.

Around ten years ago, David Wilkerson from New York, the author of 'The Cross and the Switchblade', prophesied that God would give Russia ten years – that ten years is almost up. There are indications of Communism closing in again and news of uprisings. Who knows the future? While there is freedom, we must go. In the space of nine months I went to Belarus, Malawi in Africa and also to Coimbatore in India. Here again, God is moving in a remarkable way. I went by invitation from the Prakasam brothers in Coimbatore to see the orphanages, the schools, the leper colonies and the vast church of two to three thousand people – the work God had done because Laurence Livesey and his wife went out from Blackburn, and preached for a long time without any converts. The first convert was Job. Job is the father of the Prakasam brothers; I met him, a gracious, godly, wonderful man. Until her death in October 2005, his wife of over 70 years of age still went up into the mountain villages, witnessing to the remote people about Jesus. She would travel so far in a 4x4 vehicle and then walk the rest of the way; bearing in mind there were wild animals around. Brother Job surprised me by taking an honoured crown given to him and locked in a case and publicly placed it on my head and announced, "Brother Terry, we honour you as an apostle to India." Afterwards the crown was locked up again. I felt moved by the gracious words of an outstanding man of God and the humble spirit he showed. I felt a million dollars for those five minutes! I went to the leper colony, where they rang the bell so that we and the lepers came into the building to have a short service. What joy on the faces of these people, although some had lost parts of their body which had been eaten away by that horrific disease. It is not contagious by the way! We were able to touch these people and take their little children into our arms and love them. Their rooms were only about eight foot by eight foot. That is the total capacity they had to sleep, to eat and to live, but they loved Jesus. We have some wonderful photographs of those meetings. Please pray for them.

Quite ironically, on the way out from the leper colony we saw a young couple who were worshipping snakes at the snake hill, with no hope and no God. We had just come from a worshipping, praising people who had little of this world's goods but who loved the Lord Jesus Christ.

India was another experience. I have never seen such poverty and famine in my life. I saw children chasing rats, catching them, killing them, skinning them, cooking them and eating them, living under new motorway parapets – anywhere where there was a little shelter, that's where they lived.

Many of them had no clothes at all – hundreds and thousands of people. The caste system has interrupted progress so much. The only hope is the Gospel of Jesus Christ reaching into all kinds of nations and castes and cultures. Thank God, He is doing it and many are coming to know the Lord and they are seeing the supernatural power of God in operation. There are healings, deliverances and even people raised from the dead.

India is a vast continent in need. Sponsorship of these children in orphanages and schools is a vital priority, so that they may grow up to love and to serve the Lord. However little, we can help. A little support for the leper colonies was received with such joy. Our experience of going into the Home for Widows was something else. The families in India generally look after widows. There are great, strong family ties and respect for the elderly, but some fall through the net and they are left on the roadside. These wonderful Christians take these in. They pray for ten hours a day. They just have a bed, a chair and a Bible. We called unannounced and caught them all praying. We had the joy not only of praying for them but we felt moved to ask them to pray for us. Reluctantly they came from prayer and reading, interrupted for those few moments.

What a privilege to be prostrate on the floor, together we were calling upon God for His help. As soon as we had finished, those dear women were back to the side of their beds, praying again. We did leave behind a large fresh cream gateaux which we were told was a big token of love to them. Before I left I caught a glimpse of their daily schedule hung on the wall like a timetable. I saw the schedule up on the wall, their timetable: ten hours a day they pray.

Please pray for the Prakasams, their family, and for all the needs they have in India. While there are vast numbers of people there is very little finance and there is much opposition. In that part of India strict laws have been passed. If anyone preaches and they see someone converted to Christianity their life is at risk and that of the convert.

I asked Peter what we should do when we arrived regarding these laws, and indeed before we even left for India. He said God's laws are different. He said, "You preach, we'll take care of the problems." I didn't fancy being put into a prison in India. We did preach at many services, three on a Sunday morning, each with 1,500 present, and in different languages. The harvest was plenteous, and we came back with a rejoicing heart. David has since told me they are erecting a huge building to accommodate around 10,000 right now.

Malawi in Central East Africa, is the fourth poorest country in the world. I had the joy of going to Malawi last year and will, God willing, return again. Steve and Joyce Mbwana my good friends in Bolton come from Malawi. They have come over here so that they can work, earn better money, and send the money back to keep their family, their friends and the pastors in that land. They invited me to Malawi and I saw what God is doing. Steve and his team have planted dozens of churches in Malawi and more recently in Mozambique. Steve and Joyce are fully committed to the work. They have a feeding program and can now buy maize for 38p per sack, which they are giving to the people so that they can sow the seed and reap the harvest to look after themselves and also sell a little surplus so that they have a small income to keep going. A wonderful project.

The village elders for a church have given ground. The first day I arrived we had an open-air service at three o'clock on a piece of ground in a village. Apart from the fact that twelve or fifteen came to know Jesus Christ, they were so impressed. The leaders were sat on a separate row of chairs with their trilby hats on and the best clothes they had, although most of them were ill-fitting. They donated a piece of land to build either a church or an orphanage, or both. For just a matter of two or three thousand pounds a building can be erected there in Malawi, and the desire of Steve is to have orphanages that are desperately needed in that part of Lilongwe, the capital of Malawi. He has a piece of land that has been given to him for a prayer room and a church in another part of the city. The ground has been given, the money is short, so much can be done. I felt such a burden from the Lord that I have committed myself to raise the finance to build a clinic and orphanage and sponsor 20 children initially, at £10 each per month – all under the banner of Lifeline Ministries. The project is just about completed and we have just a few more children to be sponsored. The directors have graciously named the orphanage 'The Terry and Sylvia Hanford Home'. I now have a cow named after me in India, a toilet block in Russia and an orphanage in Malawi! Children are being discarded, abortions are taking place, thousands are dying of HIV/AIDS in Africa. What can we do to stem the tide? Whatever we do in presenting Jesus as their only hope of salvation, people are hungry for the Word, but we also help in practical ways too.

After a break from broadcasting God has opened the central part of Africa to the sound of the Gospel over the air waves once more. Trans World Radio have invited Steve Mbwana and me to produce a weekly program to be aired from their new radio station in Malawi. This has now increased to three of my Gospel messages per week reaching into the surrounding countries including Mozambique, Zambia and as far as Congo. Already encouraging responses from these countries have provided openings for evangelists to go into new territory, and churches are being established because of the impact of radio. Mary and Dave Andrews record these programs in their studio adapted in a spare bedroom of their home in Bolton. Brian and Christine Roles help with scripts. I took a long trip by bus (it was supposed to have been a luxury bus but it broke down a number of times) to Blantyre, Malawi's largest city, from Lilongwe. There was a family there who invited me. The young man had visited Bolton some years ago, when the church was in Crawford Street, and Walter and Joan Owen befriended this young man. So when I went to Malawi, they were interested in me visiting them. I did so. It was a long journey and afterwards we had one meeting in darkness, except for one or two little oil lamps. To say the way to the church was rough would be an understatement. We got there in darkness. I could not see if there was a congregation or not, all I could hear were some voices praising God. I only knew there were people there when I trod on their toes but I gave an invitation for people to come out for prayer and I felt the jostling of people. This was tremendous. They want to finish that building. They have got the bricks, stones and wood outside. Bringing electricity in and building some basic facilities will soon be accomplished. Again, for a few hundred pounds that building could be completed. God help us. I know there are times when some of us Christians might spend that kind of money on almost non-entities. There are times when we feel that a little is too small. A little is much in these countries. We stayed in the colonial-type house of a government minister, a godly man. We were so glad to know that there are a number of Christians in high office in the Malawian Government. They have informed us that we can return to hold open-air services from the back of a truck and move to about six locations and preach from the truck and afterwards, for a period of time, train these young men in the ministry which they desperately need. The indigenous principle still reigns. The best people to do the work are the people from their own country, their own culture, their own language. Here we see a fruitful ministry.

It was my joy on our last trip to meet with the newly elected General Superintendent of the Assemblies of God in Malawi, Dr Lazarus Chakawara. He told me that this year they were going to be independent from the American Assemblies of God and they wanted links with other missionary bodies around the world. I was able to put David Petts and Ron Hibbert in touch with him, a visionary man who begged me to give more time to the college on my next visit and teach in the Bible school. Maybe that will happen.

It also happened in Minsk, the Capital of Belarus, for here also was a new principal, and this was the first time he had met with a British Pentecostal pastor. There is a call from all over the world and the call comes to you today: What can you do? If only I was 21 again. I came back from Malawi completely exhausted and I'm just about getting over that now. But that's another story.

God cares, God protects but He expects us to be wise.

Do not force doors open, let God open the door. The doors He opens will never shut. If we have to pull strings, you can be sure that it is not going to be fruitful. God will take you on a life of adventure if you are solely committed to Him. However great the need is, He can supply. He may test you to the last moment, be not afraid. For the God that I serve is the 'I am' – always the same, yesterday, today and forever.

There are many hills to overcome but God has given us faith and wisdom, enabling us to overcome every hill. The hill of transport, the difficulty of getting around some of these countries, has struck me with great force this last year. We have had the joy of providing several bicycles for the evangelists who are queuing up to answer the call of God to go into the villages in Malawi. These bicycles only cost £60. They are made strong with tyres that can take the difficult terrain they have to overcome. Whereas they could only walk perhaps 30 or 40 kilometres, they are now able to double and treble the area they can reach in a week. The latest statistics show that an average of 50 people for each evangelist, each week, are coming to faith in Jesus Christ. What an investment. I would like you to pray that God will help you to do what you can do to answer the call of God to go into all the world to preach the Gospel and to make disciples of all nations. There is no doubt that difficulties come and, as I mentioned previously about going through the Bronx area of New York so foolishly when I was in my 20s, this recent trip to Belarus had its scary times too. When we went down into the city of Homel, in the Chernobyl area, the local pastor decided to give the car a check up before our return journey late at night, to make sure that it would be alright for the long distance back, several hundred kilometres to where we were staying. He came and reported that there was not a drop of oil in the tank. We had probably come two or three hundred kilometres without a drop of oil in the tank at all. It took two-and-a-half litres of oil to replenish it and we started for home. On the way, in the darkness with no lamp lights or Catseyes, there was a rattling underneath the car which was a mystery to us. In fact the exhaust was damaged and our good driver had tied it up with cloth! While we were travelling along, just on the speed limit or a bit over, two policemen in yellow jackets stopped us. Our driver, Sasha, said, "Oh, I think I have gone over the speed limit, get all your papers ready," which we did. We stopped. I was always the last getting out of the car, quite slowly, when I heard shouts which were quite alarming. I could not understand what they were saying but there was an urgency about it and I got out quicker then. I got my bag and my bits and pieces and asked, "What has happened?" The cloth underneath the car had come alight. There was a naked flame just under the petrol tank. The police said that another five minutes in that car and the car and contents would have been blown up together. We would probably have gone into eternity! We felt that they were two angels, not two speed cops! They were angels when they didn't take notice of the fact that we had broken the speed limit and waved us on after they had put the flames out. Of course we now had the rattle of this broken exhaust pipe and the prospect of a couple of hundred miles with that noise. Sasha pulled into the side where there was a solitary bus hut made of a few bricks with a little bench and a small light, the only light which we could find. The kerb was high so we drove up onto the kerb so that he had room to get under the car with the little light plus torches that we had with us. We found in the back of the car a thin steel rod that was used in the summer time for their camping equipment. He managed to put the two pieces of exhaust together and we drove back home. God protects. He gives His angels charge over you. We were so conscious of that. The police told us that another five minutes in that car and we would have been dead. I noticed that when Oleg put petrol into the car he always prayed. They are all old cars – 15 to 20 years old – and not maintained or serviced. They keep them going until they break down and then put the thing right and then keep on going again. Looking into the wing mirror I could see these dear brothers praying every time as they put petrol into the tank. We were happy, of course, to cover the fuel costs, but normally they would not put much petrol in, perhaps a gallon or two, and I am convinced that those cars went further than they would normally go on such little petrol. God expanded the ability for us to cover so many miles. We were on the Lord's work and the Lord's business. Alexander Zhibrik (known as Sasha), our driver and interpreter, is an example of the fine young leaders God is raising up in Eastern Europe, and it has been my privilege to leave a legacy through time spent in training these men. A recent letter from Sasha puts it like this:

Dear Terry,

I was deeply touched by your letter. I wish I have such desire to serve the Lord as you do. I printed out your letter and I am praying about you laying my hands on it. Brother, I pray (for you), so that when time comes for you to go to the Lord you will be not in sleepers of a sick man but in the preacher's shoes, as you preached when you were here (in Belarus). I still remember that message, and I want you to know that you were and you still are a great encouragement for me in my ministry. No matter what obstacles you face, I do not look at your health conditions, Terry, I think the Lord allows me to see in you what He sees in us – our hearts. And I see that in your heart you are in the ministry, even when physically you are not there. I love you very much Terry and I miss you a lot.

Yours, Sasha. *(as written)*

When we were in Russia, we baptised converts in the Volga River, freely and without permission, something that we could not do in the UK. We erected big amplification systems to preach the Gospel in towns with no permission, we could not do that here. In Israel, we saw people rejoice in the Lord, getting saved, baptised and some of them filled with the Holy Ghost in the same day.

This is not a book in which I want to emphasise the fact that I have been to many places, but I want to tell you that Jesus can take a nobody. Jesus can give you the thrill of attaining the dream and vision that you may have. No one is too small or insignificant for God to use. It is an adventure to live for Jesus. Sometimes you go out not knowing where you are going to go, as Abraham of old, but, "the steps of a good man are ordered of the Lord." Keep your eyes open, see God's bigger picture and know that you are in it. You were chosen before the foundation of the world. Mountains may be in front of you but there is not a mountain that cannot become a hill or a hill become a plain when you go walking with the steps of a giant as you are more than a conqueror through Him that loves you. Believe it and walk in it.

When we went back to Belarus we had two wonderful testimonies proven by time and substantiated by doctors to be the work of God. A little boy who had a serious heart condition, after prayer a year ago, was wonderfully healed. A dear lady who came to one meeting asked us to pray for her neighbour who had a growth and was in a serious condition. The Lord wonderfully removed that growth and healed her. God heals. I do not believe that God puts sicknesses on people but he allows them. I believe in demon possession but I believe that the blood of Christ covers a Christian and that Satan can oppress but not possess a Christian. There is only one that lives in the heart of a born-again believer, on the throne of the heart, and that is Jesus. So Christians do have bad days. The Lord is never closer to you than when you are hurting (2 Cor. 1:3-4). You may not be able to shake off some harsh words spoken to you that have hurt you, maybe days or years ago. You may constantly battle against feelings of rejection and unworthiness, and they are huge mountains to overcome, but when you search God's Word alone, with your Bible open, the Holy Spirit speaks to you. You are overwhelmed with feelings of ignorance but Paul speaks to us through our ignorance and naivety as He spoke to Timothy about frequent illnesses. He called them 'infirmities', which means: 'sickly', 'without strength', 'feeble in body and mind'. He was referring not only to mental illness but also to those inexplicable times when feelings betray you and play tricks with your mind. Feelings of guilt, fear, anxiety and infirmities of mind because of something in the past that clings to your life. Paul was plagued with many fears (2 Cor. 7:5, 6). He was no superman.

David was a man after God's own heart. He was an adulterer and a murderer, a warrior, a musician, a prophet, a sinner and yet someone near to God's heart because repentance is such a powerful work of God. He prophesied of Jesus and resembled Him in some ways. Huge chunks of the Bible quote some of the men of the Old Testament who committed amazing sins but God raises them up, God teaches them lessons during those hard times. God did that with me, and there were others. I met a young woman from Blackpool who was in a desperate condition, physically and mentally disturbed. I talked to her about Jesus and she took Christ into her heart. Her life changed and she was soon out of hospital. She had hope, the hope of the Gospel, something we must hold precious and be prepared to share with other people. High points that readily come to mind have been the privileges of teaching and inspiring, and putting something into the hearts and lives of young men all around the world.

It was a great joy to visit Australia and see young men in their Bible schools, committed to Jesus Christ, and for me to preach in the Southern Cross Bible College in the recognition meeting, when students who were passing out of the college into the work of God received their diplomas. For the first time in my life I was dressed in a gown. The academic gown was very hot, but I will never forget that meeting which the principal, who was Aeron Morgan, my cousin, had kindly invited me to. I met Tony Hallo in Townsville and many other great men in Melbourne, in Adelaide and in different parts of that wonderful country, where we enjoyed the fellowship and the warmth of the Australian people. God's hand is upon that land and the Christian spotlight seems to have switched from America to Australia. We also felt that from Australia God's blessing was flowing into the Central Asian countries where God is moving in the vast churches and from where we can learn so much. During 2003 my visits to India, Russia and Malawi resulted in up to a thousand young people offering themselves for service in the work of God.

It has been a pleasure to travel widely in Europe with the Broadcasting Council, mainly holding seminars and rallies, promoting the use of media for the Gospel. Scandinavia and Eastern Europe, the Netherlands and adjoining countries were also visited. Ironically countries like Italy have had so much more freedom than the UK. In Rome there have been hundreds of radio stations and dozens of TV stations. We were seeking to inspire the Christian leaders to take the opportunities and happily they did so with great success. Travelling through France we would stop and meet leading brethren to share about the work. John Wildrianne would inevitably drive the hundreds of miles, after all he knew the language and also the routes. We stopped in Paris and Limoges on one trip, and those who know about my restricted diet will imagine the consternation on my face when I saw our host had prepared a delicacy of quails presented in the shape of a dome. I felt sure each little bird was looking at me, but they needed to have no fear of me devouring them. And soon a large fish was put before us with huge eyes and its mouth open. This time I shrank and felt a little like Jonah.

We proceeded through Marseilles along the magnificent French Riviera to Monte Carlo. Rome seemed the end of the world having travelled almost 20 hours by that time. But the welcome of Francesco Toppi, President of the Italian Assemblies of God, was so warm and the meetings so different and inspiring, we were soon revived. By the way, something positive happened to me when I tasted true Italian pizzas. I've been sold on them forever. Although they do taste different in Italian restaurants than from our corner shops.

On this occasion we helped with the arrangements and transport of portable homes because of the devastation left by a huge earthquake. I have never seen such carnage. Many had lost loved ones, homes were flattened and the unusual sight of cars perched perilously on concrete mountains was something I shall not forget.

When Sunday morning came hundreds of people gathered in the town centre of Lioni. I was asked to preach the Gospel and hundreds were saved. People jostled around you, all standing because there no chairs. It was bitterly cold but this did not deter these hardy people. We used the sleeping bags as extra protection from the cold. The gratitude of these people for the generosity of our British Christians made me weep. There was no sense of despair and depression. They were assisted by a small group of intrepid Christians from other countries supporting them in their need. We returned to England numb, broken hearted for those people and with a goat's cheese, the size and shape of a melon.

One time we were in Kenya where we went out to a little church which we knew nothing about and they knew nothing about us, full of black people, about ten miles out of Malindi. There was no one around when we arrived, but soon faces appeared and we were invited into the church. The pastor knew a little bit of English. We got talking and then he stopped and he said, "Just a moment, have I met you before?"

I said, "No way!"

He said, "Well, I know your voice. Have you been speaking on the 'Voice of Kenya'?

"Yes!" I said.

He said, "Well, do you know, we have a little transistor radio which we put in the middle of our group in the church. We have a little drink and a sandwich at night and you have become our pastor, our evangelist, our teacher." I was so moved. He finished, "But the radio has been stolen." Unusually for us, Sylvia was carrying a small transistor radio in her bag and she gave it to them. It was like giving a million pounds to them. And so they were able to continue being fed and helped by radio broadcasting.

Satan does not govern the airwaves. He may be the god of this age. He may rule and reign in many areas but I want to say that God's voice is above Satan's voice and that voice reaches right around the world. Friends, we must use media. 'Media' is not a frightening word, it is just a word that links by all means, from one source to another, to get the message from one side to the other, just like the early pioneers were ridiculed because they said they could speak through a wire, and across the waters someone else could hear them. Alexander Bell was put in prison because he invented a way by which sound could be transferred from one place to another through a wire. He was called a lunatic and taken away. If we had shares in the Bell Corporation in the United States right now, we would be very rich people. God has given you a vision. God has put something in your heart which is radical, you know it is of God. Overcome the mountain of your own fearfulness and timidity and go for it. The world is your parish and God can do amazing things with vessels that you might feel are useless. God can do it.

Denton Pentecostal Church provided a platform for this interest and passion of mine. They helped and supported me so much. I went to visit the Radio Manx studio and made enquiries about the possibility of hiring time to broadcast from Denton. I was greatly encouraged to know that Billy Graham's programme 'The Hour of Decision' was on their schedule. I came away so excited that we could make a humble start. I found that there were times when the broadcast could be heard on the North Lancashire coast across the water. Small acorns grow into mighty oak trees and our '**small beginnings**' went into South America and India. You will never know where God will take you. A life of adventure awaits those who are dedicated to Christ. Young people, there are ministries, there are avenues, there are places in this world for you to go to. Excitement! There is no excitement like serving Jesus and no greater joy than leading someone personally to the saving power of His grace.

It was while in Denton that I met Ian Watson for the first time. Ian was a young boy then but now has become the Senior Pastor of Bolton Pentecostal Church. Ian was gifted and a very stable, consistent and reliable lad. He went into Bible college and first served God in Burnley and now in Bolton. But in those days, Ian was our youth pastor and did a terrific job. He would I guess today be called an associate minister, and if it had not been for the limitations of faith by some men, maybe including myself, Ian could well have come back from Bible school and become part of our ministry team. As well as Ian, into the church came a great couple of stature and renown, George and Ruth Stormont, who worshipped with us for some time. I was amazed to see George, who had been the pastor of

Bethshan Tabernacle, at one time the largest church in the movement. He came to my doorstep on the first morning we arrived in Denton to welcome us. In fact, he would have come part-time into our ministry team, but again I couldn't get unity amongst the leadership with regard to a small salary. I believe that we missed something great during that period of time. George eventually went to Duluth, Minnesota, in the United States, where he ministered until he retired.

There are times and opportunities which we must not miss. We must be sensitive to God's Spirit. Some of the hills that we are to face are of rejection, are of disappointment and are of discouragement, and may be a feeling of being hindered and hampered in progress. A progressive church and a people who are willing to be led by God's Spirit is a precious thing.

In the final chapter of the book, 'Who Would Have the Nerve to Apply for Such a Post', the author makes the point that one of the toughest tasks a church faces is choosing a good minister.

In the book, a member of an official board undergoing this painful process finally lost patience. He had watched the Pastoral Relations Committee reject applicant after applicant for some fault, alleged or otherwise. It was time for a bit of soul-searching on the part of the committee. So he stood up and read a letter purporting to be from another applicant: "Gentlemen, understanding your pulpit is vacant, I should like to apply for the position. I have many qualifications. I have been a preacher of much success and also some success as a writer. Some say I am a good organiser. I have been a leader in most places I have been. I am over 50 years of age, I have never preached in one place for more than three years. In some places I have left town after my work has caused riots and disturbances. I must admit, I have been in jail three or four times but not because of any real wrong doing. My health is not too good though I still get a great deal done. The churches I have preached in have been small though located in several large cities. I have not got along well with religious leaders in towns where I have preached. In fact, some have threatened me and even attacked me physically. I am not too good at keeping records. I have been known to forget whom I have baptised. However, if you can use me I shall do my best for you." The board member looked over the committee, "What do you think, shall we call him?" The good church folks were aghast. Call an unhealthy, troublemaking, absent-minded, ex-jail bird? Was the board member crazy? Who signed that application? Who had such colossal nerve? The board member eyed them all keenly before he answered, "It is signed, the Apostle Paul."

(Author unknown, submitted by Rev C W Kirkpatrick, Union Church of Christ, Ludlow, England).

CHAPTER EIGHT

Pioneering at 50?

It was a difficult time when we came to the end of our ministry at Denton. After 13 wonderful and happy years, having seen the work blessed and increased, Pastor Jim Bowler took on the pastorate. We wondered which way God was going to take us.

After some months and a lot of persuasion we began to look after a group of people in Hyde, the next town. For many years, we had had our eye on that town of Hyde. In fact the Assemblies of God in this area had started in Hyde back in the days of Alfred Webb who was born in the town. The building we now have today for God's work in Hyde was originally an Assembly of God, but when Alfred left for Dagenham he left behind Mr Barber, who became pastor of the church and took it out of Assemblies of God.

At Denton we had always had a great interest in the town of Hyde, which was four or five miles away. However, there had not been a work there for many years. Every time I went to the General Conference, Alfred would say to me, "Terry, when are you going to start a work in Hyde?" The answer was always the same: "In God's time, at God's bidding."

The sudden tragic deaths of David Newton and Michael Thomas, two young men, hurt me. David was a successful student at Manchester's top school. Michael was a shade younger. I had played darts with him just a few days before. It was almost like the loss we felt when Fred Fletcher died a few years after we arrived in Denton. Fred and his wife, Lily, had served God in the pastorate of Swinton Assembly until Fred suffered a stroke. They were great practical and faithful servants of God and friends of ours. Fred loved to babysit for us but found that our son, Jason, was quite a handful. On one occasion they were playing with handcuffs and Jason had put them on Uncle Fred and had lost the key! We had a slight dilemma when eventually we returned to their home after a long prayer meeting. Fred was greatly restricted until we sorted matters out. Fred was so good to Sharon and Jason; it compensated our children for the trauma of leaving Exeter and their friends. Although handicapped, Fred played with them and laughed with them. One of my greatest joys was to appoint Fred an elder in the Assembly in Denton, because I felt that certain people are of the opinion that handicapped people are affected mentally. Fred was handicapped physically but he had so much spiritual wisdom to give and was an asset to the church. Lily has maintained her service for the Lord faithfully through the years, although losing her sister was a blow to us all. Gladys had come back to the Lord while we pastored in Denton.

Hyde

The dream of Alf Webb came to pass. We did not think it would happen the way it did but God's ways are past finding out. A number of people, who left the Denton Assembly and did not quite know which way to go at that time, met together in a school in Hyde. After a special meeting that they called they asked if I would come and meet with them. They wanted a shepherd and I wanted people. After about three months we decided to commence a pioneer work in Hyde. Bear in mind that we were deeply involved in the pioneering of a new church in Woodley in its infancy with Colin Carson, its leader. Woodley is about four miles towards Stockport. In Hyde we used the school, the town hall, a small cooperative hall, and whatever we could hire. They were difficult times, as we had to bring the hymn books, the electric organ, the overhead projector and everything else that we required. We started with nothing, but as money was given we would use it to buy the necessary equipment. God helped us and people were saved and healed and backsliders were restored. We had some wonderful meetings at that time in the town hall, which would hold 600 people; we would have possibly a maximum of 120 people on a Sunday night. In the small co-operative hall we would have about 60 people jammed into one room. The town hall was expensive as it was over £100 every time we hired it. We had no funds but the people began to give generously and they were able to support me to an extent and pay our bills. We wanted a hall of our own. Was there one?

There was a little prefabricated building on Crook Street that was owned by the Manchester City Mission. It was not a very good building at all as it was rusty, breaking down and letting in water. There were just one or two people still attending the Mission and the pastor was elderly and about to give up. After quite some time of negotiation, the Manchester City Mission decided to sell the building to us for about £12,000. We were glad to have our own place. We renovated it, spent money on it and made it look more presentable. There was also a little piece of land with the building and so, in time, we bought two Portakabins for the Sunday school and extra toilet facilities. We did what we could. There was also a baptistry there, of a sort. We baptised many converts right there in that old building. In fact, in one baptismal service, we had 168 people in a building that normally would only fit about 60. How we did it I do not know. There was a little side room which we knocked down to enlarge the building just a little. It was ancient, really uninviting for the 20th century, but it was ours and we saw God move in that place. Difficulties abounded, people who said that they would stick with the work and see us through forsook us and fled as they did Jesus. People had said that they would be with us through any circumstance: "We will stand with you, Terry!" The disappointment, the discouragement, the depression was something which I would not wish on anyone.

I also want to mention the highlights. We had weddings and funeral services, dedication services, convention meetings, good preachers, fine fellowship and we just want to thank God for every person that came to know Jesus in those years. We had a people with a great desire to reach out into the town through open-air meetings, using the market area stalls, where we would sell second-hand goods and give away things and where we would witness for Jesus, using drama groups with young people of passion and ability. In fact, out of that work of the Lord some who are now serving God full-time here and abroad heard God calling them.

Hyde has become a notorious town because, since those days of course, we have had the saga of Dr Shipman, the greatest mass murderer of all time, who had his surgery in town. My wife, Sylvia, worked in the health service and knew him well. He seemed a fine man but when the news came out of his crimes we could not believe it. Hyde was put on the map. The time came when, through ill health, I landed in hospital, three times with nervous breakdowns.

That temporary building has been sold to a garage next-door and the building has been demolished. The land was only worth around £20,000 but it was more than we had paid for the building, and with the £20,000 and more the church that was originally the Assembly of God has been bought back. The church was greatly helped by a legacy left for them which came at the right time, so the work continues but needs much prayer and especially for the leadership. One thing we would remember with great humour, and solemnity too, is that when we put a new floor into the building we discovered that the church had been built on top of a small burial plot and several headstones were still left flattened in the foundation rubble! We did look for people coming alive in Christ Jesus, transformed by the power of God and becoming great lively witnesses in that town, but this discovery was bewildering.

We thank God for the loyalty and faithfulness of good people. I believe that this is noted in heaven and I think particularly of Lily Fletcher, Helen Scott, Pat and Peter Birchenough and others. God is breaking through in a new way in these days, where there are men of vision and men and women prepared to work and witness. I pray that Hyde will become a shining example of what God can do with a small number of people and build up yet again, a strong Pentecostal witness in that needy town of Hyde in Cheshire. We may have seen 168 people crammed in the old building at a baptismal service, but we always recognised that the Glory of God on the house and the preaching of the Gospel with signs following was of paramount importance.

Some extracts from letters received, all glory to God.

From Alex (Sasha) Zhibrik, Belarus:
"Brother Terry, I still remember that message you preached, and I want you to know that you were and are still a great encouragement to me in my ministry, no matter what obstacles you face, I do not look at your health conditions, Terry, I think the Lord allows me to see in you what He sees in us; our hearts. And I see that in your heart you are in the ministry, even when physically you are not there. I love you very much Terry and I miss you a lot. Yours, Sasha.

From the General Secretary, God's Mission International, Malawi, Africa:
"We give thanks to God for you enabled us to launch Operation Soul Winning Project in June when you, Pastor Terry, visited us. You were the first to donate funds for the bicycles for this project. We started with four Evangelists with one bicycle each. We have now sent out 17. About 80 people were saved the first week. We have recently sent four into Mozambique where up to 5,000 attend the Gospel services."

From Yevgenly Sergeyenia, Gomel, Belarus:
"Thank you for coming to my region where few venture following the huge radiation explosion. You are the first British preacher to venture because many fear

the after-effects of the nuclear explosion. The meeting was packed with people with many saved, many filled with the Spirit and healed. We wish you would come again for a longer period."

From Peter and David Prakasam,
Coimbatore, South India:
"I thank you so much for remembering us. Thank you for your loving letter. Every day I think of your message to our pastors. I have never in my life heard such a nice message. You must come again and teach our leaders one more time. My dad, Job Prakasam, sends his love and blessing and all my family. We are extending our church building to hold 10,000. Pray for us. Even then it will be too small."

The Prakasams' father was the first convert of Brother and Sister Livesey, the first AoG missionaries from Blackburn in Britain to India.

From Pastor K T Stanley, Minsk:
"We saw a true powerful move of the Holy Spirit during the meetings with Terry and Barry. People were delivered from sin and received Jesus as Saviour. Many received healing, some delivered from evil spirits, demonic possession, evil spells and black magic."

From Oleg Dudnik, Samara, Russia:
"Without your help our church would not be completed. We were very discouraged. Now people have been saved and we believe for a strong church. God sent you to us and I pray He will do it again."

CHAPTER NINE

Trophimus, or was it Terry, I left sick? (2 Tim. 4:20)

From my early days I had many sicknesses and I just about remember going into hospital with diphtheria at the time when the Second World War broke out. While I was in hospital I got to know quite a few American soldiers who had come over to Britain, and we were always glad to see them because they brought with them some extra supplies, some sweets and chewing gum, which they would distribute among the children. I also developed pneumonia which caused me to be seriously ill for some time, but God was gracious and I did get well after giving my family another scare. My American friends bought me a tent to encourage me to make progress and want to get home. It did seem that the one who was in journeys oft, was also in sickness oft, but I never allowed sickness, infirmity or handicap of any kind to stop my vision for the future and the fulfilling of my destiny in God.

Many times God allows us to go through strange circumstances and I guess that because of a scarcity of strong and gifted men and women around me in those pioneering days it took its toll on my health. Anyone visiting the town and attending our church was an encouragement. When Ron and Faye Hopkins and Alan and Phyllis Griffiths came to a meeting we held in the town hall my heart jumped for joy, these were old friends and their stay brought great blessing to all. If it were not for the support of my wonderful wife,

Sylvia, I guess I would have given up after this particular period in my life. After nine years pioneering in Hyde I landed in hospital again. That's another story of the grace of God.

When I went into Bible college at 18 years of age, during my first term I was rushed into Redhill Hospital with peritonitis; poison was beginning to seep into my system. Again, maybe Satan tried to thwart my call or maybe God was teaching me some lessons. I related this previously. When I was 21 and in my first pastorate, I got married. Those were the days when, for the sake of respectability, one waited until the age of 21 to marry. I was married the day after my 21st birthday, I didn't waste any time! God had undoubtedly called us together and I wanted Sylvia to be at my side.

She joined me after one year of pastoring in the Peterborough Assembly. Then I was diagnosed with tuberculosis. This was treated at home. Each day for months the district nurse called to give me medication, which included injections and those dreadful streptomycin tablets. They were round and the size of a 50p piece, shaped like flying saucers. They had to be dipped in water, made so that they became soggy and easier to swallow and far more prone to make you feel sickly. Again God brought me through that. I did not realise the seriousness of my condition at that time. It was far into the future, when Sylvia became a medical secretary and my notes disclosed what condition I was in. Satan does seek to hinder but the stout spirit that God has given to me and my faith in God's grace has brought me through. Several other hospital visits followed. Collapsing on pulpits distressed me, preaching when pain was intense in my body, especially my kidneys which almost forced me to bang my head against the bedroom wall. It could happen about every seven years the doctor told me. It seemed his 'prophecy' came to pass.

Many things happened in between times, trips to hospital for various operations on my nose and a hernia operation. How good God is and how mysterious.

In 1993 I was advised to visit a specialist in London because I was manifesting the signs of Parkinson's disease, or was it Essential Tremor. Tests were inconclusive. After a period of time I saw Mr Richardson, a top neurosurgeon in Manchester and after considerable tests I received a stereotactic thalamotomy. This is a long, intricate surgical operation where a hole was bored into my skull so that the nerves in the brain causing the excessive shaking could be cauterised. This was performed on the brain while I was awake, with around ten doctors and nurses present to monitor every part of my body, e.g. each toe and finger etc. The skill of Mr Richardson, the neurosurgeon was amazing. The extreme shaking in my left arm immediately stopped and several hours later when I was taken back to my ward, a crescendo of shouts went up from the other patients as they saw the amazing improvement. I feel that an enemy, the devil himself, has tried at every vital period of my life to hinder or stop me serving Jesus. I have been determined to prove him a loser and Jesus victorious. Nothing must stop us serving Jesus. Each Christian is called to be an overcomer, whatever we face.

I used to feel that if I broke my leg or my arm I would know that after a period of time I would be well again. But being depressed and cast down, people cannot see it. To tell such people to "pull yourself together", "pick yourself up", is a thing you cannot do, it is unhelpful. Begin to pour in the Word of God, begin to pray, and begin to believe for such people, that He will do it. There are breakdowns today that have been caused by people, and there are breakdowns that God uses. It is a stigma. I felt it was a stigma, I did not want to meet people, I felt that I was marked like a leper. But when I was prepared to pull the shutters back and let the façade drop, and I mentioned that I had been afflicted by this nervous breakdown, people would come up to me from all over the place whenever I preached and say, "Thank you, Terry, for being honest and open," and so many have been helped. So many have been brought through horrendous situations simply because we are prepared to show ourselves as we are. We are not supermen. We are servants of the living God. The call of God is upon our lives but we are human, we live in the real world and it is a fallacy to tell people who come to Christ that everything will work out well and right. All things work together for good, and that means bad things and good things to those that love God and are called according to His purpose, as Romans 8 tells us. It does not mean that we are immune from problems. When we learn about God, we are taught deep lessons. Without a break the Lord has enabled me to attend the General Conference of Assemblies of God for 50 years, avoiding every hospital visit.

While flying to Spain to visit our son in autumn of 2004 I was taken ill and was moved to the back seat where oxygen was given to me. I felt extremely weak and ill, and breathing became difficult. The cabin staff of Excel Airways were very helpful and medical help was arranged as we arrived at Alicante Airport. I was taken off the plane in a wheelchair. Jason turned colour when he saw me in this state and Sylvia was extremely worried. We were asked if I wanted to go to hospital. I declined, feeling that a week's rest would probably revive me. I didn't feel excited about going into hospital in a foreign country. I thought it might be better to telephone my consultant in Manchester for his advice, bearing in mind that he had placed me on new medication prior to flying and possibly this was part of the problem. He had told us that, ideally, I should be monitored, but it would do me no harm to go on holiday. When we talked to him by phone he advised me to drop the new medication immediately. Arrangements were made for us to fly back early, but again the thought of a week in the sunshine swayed our decision to stay. We were in an apartment with fine hosts who were from Bolton and they did everything to help us. I was so weak I could not dress myself, I could only with difficulty lift a knife and fork. I could not sleep properly and most nights I had nightmares. Sylvia and Jason looked after me so well and made all preparations for first-class treatment for our return journey to Manchester. The airline was prepared with extra oxygen on board and medical expertise. Gratefully none were needed. Glad to be home, I soon saw my consultant when it was agreed that the change of medication caused the blip, but that I had not been well because the missions to Africa,

India and Russia were planned in such a short period of time.

However, because Parkinson's disease is a degenerative disease and it has finally been confirmed that this is what I have, gradually my right arm has been progressively shaking badly and daily bouts of extreme weakness are occurring. When this happens I begin to mumble my words, shuffle my feet and lose some sense of balance. Medication helps somewhat and I time my 'working hours' to fit in with the better periods of the day. I have curtailed my preaching engagements, but God wonderfully restores my speech and memory when I stand to open the Word of God, however, I am rather 'washed out' afterwards. As of 2006 I am anticipating major surgery, called Deep Brain Stimulation, which is a type of pacemaker placed under the skin and a remote control given to minimise the shaking. There is always the risk of a stroke with complex operations. This one takes seven to eight hours under anaesthetic. This surgical procedure is under discussion as I have kidney stones at the moment which require hospitalisation.

What the future holds we do not know. My life is in His hands and He cares for you and me. I am however able to record my Gospel messages for Trans World Radio every couple of weeks when I do ten each session at a time in the morning when I am at my best. Dave and Mary Andrews are so helpful with their top class studio in a bedroom. Sickness, infirmity and whatever God permits cannot stop me fulfilling His purposes. These programmes reach so many countries in Central Africa, the response is tremendous, churches are being planted and evangelists from Malawi are following up the responses. We help by supplying them with bicycles. Seventeen to date. Five now used in Mozambique. Each evangelist reports around 50 confessions for Christ each week.

My walking ability has been curtailed by the knee replacement joint I received early in 2004 after three attempts at surgery. The anaesthetic did me no favours with my other condition, but I can now walk short distances with no pain. In the early '90s I went into Cheadle Royal Hospital twice and then the Priory Hospital on another occasion. God had undoubtedly looked into the future for me. In Denton one year, instead of taking the rise in salary, I was given the opportunity to make the decision whether to take a rise or to become registered with BUPA, a private medical company. I took the second option. I have since enjoyed the services of BUPA for many years although the premiums as you get older become astronomically high. Yet we are convinced that I have probably had my money's worth back. They were very dark, dismal days in the Priory. The Priory is there for people with great nervous needs, breakdowns, addictions, and you mix with people with all kinds of needs.

God brought into my life one man who was zealous to know more about God, more about Jesus and more about His Word, and remains today a very close friend, called Peter Yates, a Christian businessman, a man who had come to a standstill in his life because of the pressures of work. He owned garden centres. The pressure had driven him into hospital in a very poor state. Very often the matron reprimanded us because we went past 'lights out' time which was 10.30 at night, talking about the Word of God and Jesus. The matron would tell us that if we did not behave ourselves, we would be sent home and that we must obey the rules of the hospital. Tablets were to be taken at ten o'clock and then lights out at 10.30. We would spend time up to midnight discussing the Word of God. Peter tells me that those times have changed his life forever. Peter is a member of an Anglican church in Lower Peover, and he is on the church council there, but also after our time together he became a member of Altrincham Baptist Church, where he has grown in the things of God. It might seem very strange that he is a member of two churches, which is not strictly allowed, but he remains with his links to Lower Peover because he believes that he is a witness for Jesus, and a born-again believer who may be able to influence that church towards more of God's commission to the Church and to the purpose of the Church these days. He draws spiritual food from the church in Altrincham. We have remained friends for many years ever since that time.

There were times when I was in my own room in the

corner, that I felt God had forsaken me and that I would never preach again, or face people again; in fact the people who visited me became a great burden to me. People would travel distances and I appreciated them coming but I did not really want to meet people. If you have ever been in the black hole of depression you can sympathise with Hannah (1 Sam. 1-2:21). Unfaithfulness and family problems drove her to the brink of disaster. The beginning of her recovery was when she stopped, "looking downward, which makes you dizzy," and began looking upward to Jesus. The upward look takes away our fear. Even literally walking with your head up high and straightening your back helps. Also at that time God was doing something within me. He was giving me compassion, teaching me lessons, teaching me that I should stop and take rest. I had been brought up on the old principles when I was young, some good and some not so good. How can I take a day off a week when I am serving God full-time? I found out in later life, to my cost, that this was not good thinking. People said never take out a pension because Jesus is coming soon. This was bad advice! Yes, Jesus is coming, however, we need to be realistic and appreciate that we have to make provision to meet our 'day-to-day' financial commitments. There were other principles which were current years ago, some may not have had a Scriptural basis, but others stood us in good stead. It was said by many, even some from the pulpit, that, "man would never walk on the moon," but we have seen it in our lifetime. We should be careful in what we say, and be sure that the Word of God substantiates it. We must always be careful to ensure that any utterances attributed to the Holy Spirit are in accord with the Bible. David the psalmist says, in Psalm 119:71: "It is good for me that I have been afflicted; that I might learn thy statutes." The Hebrew word for 'affliction' here means 'brow-beaten, troubled, abased, chastened, defiled, hurt, humbled, weakened and depressed'. When you put this meaning into the verse, suddenly it reads, "It is good for me to have been brow-beaten, troubled, abased, chastened, defiled, hurt and depressed," and it has all been for one purpose, so that I could know the

Lord's statutes. The word 'statutes' means 'engraved law'. It is good that I went through all these troubles because in the process God was engraving His laws and ways in my heart. So it is true that the Lord allows trials to come our way to test us, but that is not His primary purpose in allowing them. They are to teach us to walk upright before Him. The Bible tells us that "many are the afflictions of the righteous: but the LORD delivereth him out of them all." According to the psalmist in Psalm 34:19, He can do anything. In fact, we have seen Him fulfil that promise.

Who knows when you plant the seed what harvest is going to come? Fruit will grow where you have planted the seed. We must by all means win some. We must take every opportunity of reaching out for Jesus. Shine where you are. Overcome the difficulties of prejudice, apathy and indifference. Know that different people have different ideas and different methods but God's methods are men and women. You are the answer. There is no doubt in my mind that it is an exciting life to live for Jesus, to be led by His Holy Spirit, to be motivated with a pure motive for the glory of God, to live through days and times when you hear with sadness of men of high-ranking falling. By grace we are what we are and only by grace do we stand. Keep your eyes on Jesus.

Compounded with this is Sylvia's diagnosis of diabetes and the sudden viral attack on the inner ear which has caused her deafness in one ear, which nothing can be done about medically. We are trusting God for healing but know His Grace is sufficient, whatever happens. God's Grace and strength alone have enabled Sylvia to face these trying times. She is a marvellous wife and our love grows stronger each day. We have been married since 1957 and we thank God for each other daily. The prayer support of many around the world sustains us and my aged mother (93) and aunt (85) have always joined us in this great Christian faith.

You cannot deliver yourself out of any affliction. That is God's work. No matter what kind of trouble you are in, you simply cannot extricate yourself by your own power. The secret is to understand how God is dealing with you and as

God delivered Israel from their bondage, so he will deliver you. Now all these things happened to the children of Israel as examples. "They are written for our admonition, upon whom the ends of the world are come" (1 Corinthians 10:11). Verse six says, "Now these things became our examples." Everything that happened to Israel, their bondage, their trials, their deliverance out of Egypt are testimonies, patterns and examples to us today.

Indeed Israel's physical deliverance represents the spiritual deliverance that we are to see. Have you ever wondered why Israel did not rise up in rebellion when in bondage under Pharaoh? After all, they were fortunate to make bricks without straw. He was commanding his taskmasters to beat them. Why didn't Israel take matters into their own hands? They certainly had the manpower to do it, especially after the ten plagues when Egypt was devastated, weak and in mourning. Even Pharaoh said, "The children of Israel are more and mightier than we" (Exodus 1:9). But Israel was complacent. Even though they were suffering they still enjoyed the pleasures of Egypt. They were out of touch with God, had no vision for their future, and were prepared to settle for the status quo.

There came a time when I was recovering. I asked myself, 'Terry, what do you want to do at this period of life? You are well up in your 50s and approaching 60.' Again, people had told me in my middle 50s to ease off but I had gone out under God's bidding to pioneer and now they were saying maybe take early retirement. I want to die with my boots on, not carpet slippers, not sitting in a nice armchair in the corner of the room. I asked myself at this point, what do you really want to do for the remainder of your life, ideally?

CHAPTER TEN

Bolton or bust

Not too far away from where I was in the Priory at Altrincham was the thriving assembly at Bolton, pastored by Ian Watson who was once our youth leader in the Denton church, and I knew that the Bolton church was growing. I thought, wouldn't it be wonderful just to be a helper in that situation. To stand at the side of Ian... But that was just a dream. I thought it would never come to pass. Day by day I prayed and kept it to myself. The Lord one day indelibly spoke into my spirit: "The desires of your heart shall be fulfilled."

When Ian came to visit me in hospital something remarkable happened. Bear in mind we had never lived in each other's pockets. For several years we had gone our own ways, serving God. Ian went into Bible college and then went to Burnley and now was Pastor at Bolton. He came to see me with a message from the elders putting a proposition before me. He said, "Will you take a month to pray, Terry? See if the Lord will just lead you to come and join me in my team to major on Bible teaching."

I broke down. I was so emotionally moved, I said, "Ian, I do not have to pray for a month. God has already done a work in my heart and told me what I would be doing for the next few years." He was as surprised as I was. As soon as I came out of hospital we made plans to move to Bolton. How gracious Pastor Watson and the leadership at Bolton were: "Just do as much as you want to do and when you want to do it. Don't overtax yourself, but we want the benefit of your experience and ministry," they told me.

Paul in the Bible tells us that wherever he was, whatever condition he was in, he witnessed for the Lord, even when he was in chains in prison he still witnessed for Jesus. There are perhaps few that can adjust to being 'second or third fiddle' after pastoring for nearly 40 years. I had no desire to take a higher position again in God's Church.

Bolton

So, in 1994, we came to Bolton and there I mainly looked after the teaching ministry of the church. I prepared study outlines for the care group leaders. We had 22 groups. It has been a great joy to see some of the house group leaders feel the call of God upon their lives and that they are now in full-time ministry. The privilege of seeing young men like Phil Worsley, Darren Durham and Julian Wolstencroft etc, who I spent many hours with seeking to help them prepare for their future ministry.

As part of my ministerial mandate we were praying that God would open up this country more and more, and that God would bless every effort of Vision, Premier Radio and the God Channel for the proclamation of the Gospel; to see the media released so that we would be able to reach people where they are in their homes. God brought together many Christians who were interested in the media from around the area. On two occasions we were able to broadcast for 24 hours a day for 28 days. It was very costly, but then money spent to reach people is always money well spent.

The main priority of media ministry is to reach the most people, in the quickest time, at the lowest relative cost. There was a time when I stood on a mountain near Rivington overlooking the whole town of Bolton, and there I had a great burden for the people who were behind the closed doors and closed windows, who had never darkened the door of a church. God loves the people of this area. We began assembling the team and producing the programmes. We had the joy of using a fully equipped top professional studio, at

Claremont Chapel in Bolton, whose studio was owned by David Kangus and freely made available to us together with his professional expertise. We also received great cooperation from the Chapel and the support of many other churches. As a result we had two outreaches in two years by radio to the town of Bolton. From this outreach the God Channel snapped up three members who worked with the team, and two of them still work with them. So we do feel that fruit has resulted from that outreach. People were saved, people were contacted, people were touched in their bodies as we prayed for the sick. Many people who had some passion and burden for this work joined with us, and God brought together a lovely bonding of several people, a dedicated team to do 24-hour broadcasting. God deepened the call in many lives. Rick Brocklesby and Don Heginbotham still work with the God Channel. That was a most marked occasion in the life of our ministry in Bolton Pentecostal Church. It cost around about £7,000 a time. It was not cheap going but without the help of a ready-made studio it would have cost far more. But who can put a value on a soul coming to know Jesus, and it is essential that we understand that we must be out where the sinners are.

One thing I always remember American evangelist T L Osborne saying is that, "You don't catch fish in swimming pools." We must go out where the fish are. This dominates my life even now. I can feel it in my bones. We must reach people wherever they are by all means.

Undoubtedly one of the happiest days of my life was when my father gave his life to Christ. From the time I learned to pray as a young boy, and for most of my life, I prayed for my dad. He was a good man but it was very difficult to talk to him about Jesus. One day, when he was in his 80s and not in good health, he was lying on his bed at home. I had gone down to visit my parents for the day. After I had left and I had gone about 40 miles on my journey back to Manchester, speeding up the motorway, I heard God speak into my spirit: "Well, you are not a very fine Christian are you? You left home and did not even pray with your mum and dad." I used to feel that I would embarrass my father if I did. Anyway, I turned round and went back. I told my mum that there was nothing wrong with the car. I asked her to make Dad a cup of tea and said that I would take it up to him.

"But I have just taken him one," she said.

"I'll take him another one," I said to Mum, which was just an excuse to talk to Dad. I said, "Dad, I haven't come back because there is some difficulty or the car has broken down," which he thought it might have done. "I just want to ask you, isn't it about time you gave your life to Jesus?"

For the first time in his life he said, "Yes," and the tears began to trickle down his cheeks. I led him through the sinner's prayer and I believe that Jesus came into his heart and life that day. His mind was crystal clear at that time and he knew exactly what was happening. Mum came up to the room and I told her what had happened before I left and returned to Manchester. When I got back to Manchester I rang them to tell them I had got home safe and to find out what had happened after I had left. My mother told me that she had wanted to make sure and so she had also led Dad through the sinner's prayer. From that time on until Dad went to heaven, they prayed together, linked little fingers together in bed and prayed the Lord's Prayer.

I believe that was the day when the great transaction was done. Never give up praying, never give in, however many years it takes. I prayed from being a very young child, every day. I believe that the promise of God should be held onto: "You will be saved, you and your household" (Acts 16:31). We are believing for backsliders in our families to be restored, and for those who do not know Jesus as Saviour to come to know Him. Never give up, always believe, take advantage of all the opportunities which come your way to witness, for the time is short and urgency must beat in our hearts. It really is a matter of life or death (Ezek. 33:7-9).

It was a great joy to see two of my father's sisters give their lives to Jesus at the funeral service, and they have formed an evangelical Anglican church near their homes in Swansea.

CHAPTER ELEVEN

Serving others

The opportunity of holding certain positions in Assemblies of God has helped me, but I have never been one who has looked for them. Every district council (now known as regional councils) on which I have served, I have served God to the best of my ability, whether that be as Home Missions Secretary, Secretary to the District, District Chairman, being on the Broadcasting Committee, the Resolutions Committee or other bodies both locally, nationally and internationally. This led to the breakthrough, especially in broadcasting, and the opportunity of visiting many European countries, and particularly in planting into hearts the vision, purpose and passion of reaching people for Christ, always bearing in mind what remains in my heart today – to be out where the sinners are. People are behind their curtains, behind their front doors or in bingo halls or wherever they congregate. We must, by all means, win some.

For many years I had the privilege of serving on the Board of Directors of Christian Solidarity International, a Christian human rights organisation. Campaigning on behalf of Christians worldwide who have been unjustly imprisoned for their Christian beliefs has been the main thrust of the organisation. This has also given me the privilege of meeting national leaders and Members of Parliament from both the House of Lords and the House of Commons. A particular privilege was to meet Lord Tonypandy, George Thomas; to stand at his side and sing some great Welsh hymns was a real honour. To hear of Christians being released from prison was our reward. I did organise prayer support groups in our area for this work, and the Deputy Speaker of the House of Lords at the time, Lady Caroline Cox (now Baroness Cox), came to speak in our church which was packed for this historic meeting. A huge offering was given to this worthy cause.

The pressure of work and having to travel to London for the meetings eventually proved too much and, with great regret, I resigned. However I feel honoured to have proposed Stuart Windsor as National Director when the vacancy arose some years ago. He was God's man for the moment and has been very successful in that appointment. For many years I served as a member of the Sussex Youth Camps Committee. This brought untold blessing. Under the directorship of Peter Butt, we saw literally hundreds of young people filled with the Holy Spirit, saved, healed and called of God into His service. Even now I meet people around the country who tell me that those camp weeks made a huge difference in the course of their personal spiritual destiny. Great Walstead School and other venues became a meeting place with God. Personal memories of mighty anointings on our ministry will never be forgotten. Late into the night we would be counselling young folk and guiding them as best we knew. I also helped raise funds for a more permanent building, and donated all gifts for my first booklet to that cause.

Another poem by Joan Nichols, 'The Bridge' Church

Oh Terry, just open your eyes... can't you see
That around you the sky brightly shines with the angelic host
I've assigned 'just for you',
Protecting and keeping and generally bringing you through
Trial and testing.

Anxiety shouts in your ear... "FEAR what's going to be."
While My Spirit within you says, "Rest, son, in Me."
Just think of the places you've been and the hardships you've known,
Well, this season's a harvest for you to reap all that you've sown,
My blessings are pouring; My favour surrounds all you are,
Do you doubt I can keep what I've sovereignly nurtured this far?
You've given so much and 'spent' who you are, serving Me,
Do you think I've been 'phased' or surprised by this troublesome knee?
I throw back My head and I laugh at what flits through your head,
I knit you together; I'll work this for good like I've said,
Terry, know that the voice of the saints rise before Me in prayer,
That the vast heavenly host and My Spirit... are already there.

CHAPTER TWELVE

Lessons learned

What a great life it is serving Jesus! Having served for 47 years in pastoral work I can thank God for every moment, every joy and (yes!) every problem. Wouldn't it be wonderful if the following reflected a typical day in our lives:

> *"You know it is going to be a good day when you wake up and your wife has already put the coffee on. When the paper boy puts the paper on the porch, when the children get ready for school the first time you call them, when you don't burn the toast, when a friend calls and invites you to lunch, when the first babysitter you call says 'yes'. When you hit the shopping centre and find an unadvertised sale and there is money in your pocket, when you find a parking space right next to the shop door. When your husband comes home from work and gives you an unexpected compliment, when you are the first at the supermarket checkout queue, when no bills arrive in the post, when the credit card company sends you a cheque for overpayment, when the car doesn't need a tank of petrol just for errands, when someone tells you that you are their best friend, when you receive a happy anniversary or birthday card from your husband without having to drop any hints, when God answers your prayers, when the kids offer to do the dishes, when the laundry basket is empty, when all the household appliances are working satisfactorily, when both of your toddlers take naps at the same*

> *time, when the children pick up the toys without being asked to, when someone calls and invites all your kids over to play for the afternoon, when your husband takes out the rubbish, when the family leaves enough hot water for your bath, when you can blow up a balloon with air to spare, when your family tells you how much they love you, you know it is going to be a good day.*
> *(Submitted by Gail Jones)*

I believe that I will be misunderstood for saying this, but I hope you can understand: if you can keep out of the ministry, keep out. I say this because too many today are treating the ministry as an alternative occupation. The call of God on your life means that you will never be fulfilled in any other direction. However, if the call of God is not there, don't start. There is no 'plan B' when God calls. You cannot spin some cosmic coin and that will decide which way you will go. There will be times when you stand alone with only your call to keep you going. There will be times when you are left with nothing and nobody. There will be people who will say that they will never leave you, that they will stand with you and stay by your side, but some of these will go. However, the call of God will still burn within you and the promises of God will be your security. Your destiny is marked, you cannot go any other way. Discipline in study, consistency in devotion, faithfulness to the task will see you through.

Your personal call is important

I believe that the Word of God has promises, and promises personally to you need to be kept hidden in your heart. Do remember that it may take a long time for the promises to be fulfilled but they will be, however outrageous they may be. When God gave me the promise in Psalm 19:4 – "Their line shall go out throughout all the earth and their words to the end of the world." I did not know what this meant, it was impossible! Years later, God gave me that opportunity to broadcast around the world. God is faithful. He has a destiny for you. You must find it, know it and walk in it day-by-day.

The first lesson that I have learned which is of paramount importance is that servanthood and sacrifice is the lifestyle of those who will be successful in God. I do not mean that we will always be depressed and negative, far from it. Some people go around as if it is a gift of the Spirit. Sacrifice and a servant spirit is a joyful, fulfilling, wonderful attitude that God looks for in those who will serve Him. It does not mean that you will always be poor. The most I ever received in the work of God was £200 a week but I tell you that God is faithful. There will be times when you have much and times when you have little. When you can say, "blessed be the name of the Lord," that is a tremendous acknowledgement of God's faithfulness. Don't serve God for filthy lucre (1 Tim. 3:8 AV), but if you have a spirit of adventure God will enable you to fulfil the desires of your heart. God has privileged me to see quite a bit of this world, five continents and 70 countries, but so what. If I go just to look at places and to say that I have been to another country, what will it count in heaven? I want to go where the need is. I want to go, however poor the country is, and for most of my missions I have had to believe God for every penny that it cost. I have talked to thousands of leaders and seen the joy of over 30 people in full-time ministry today, and yet how small an accomplishment that is in the light of the number of opportunities given to me. With opportunity there comes responsibility. I have learned that servanthood, sacrifice in spirit and lifestyle bring huge rewards. For this of course, one must be filled with the Spirit. We must be people of prayer. If we don't have regular trips to the 'Upper Room' we may just become froth-blowers, but we need to be men full of the Holy Spirit.

Secondly, if you have ever seen a husband trying to solve the dilemma of a growing family all by himself, or a wife trying to do it all by herself, you will get some idea of how a pastor or Christian leader goes wrong when he tries to solve local church problems by himself. It takes a team to be really successful. In a marriage, it takes husbands who love their wives and wives who are loving helpmates to their husbands. It takes both of them, working, growing, praying, growing together and, "submitting to one another in the fear of God" (Eph. 5:21). Administrating the problems of local churches successfully, especially growing churches, makes team ministry virtually mandatory. This was perhaps not possible in the early days of ministry, but for these days I believe that a team is absolutely necessary. The members of the team would be equals but would have a leader amongst equals. The sky is the limit. The idea of building a team ministry that enables churches to grow, perhaps even to astronomical sizes, was thought impossible some years ago but is increasingly desirable in an urban society in the days in which we live.

Another lesson: learn to sit where people sit (Ezek. 3:15-17). Be a people person. Care for the flock. Feed the flock, lead the flock and lead them to maturity. It says in Psalm 19:4: "Their line has gone out through all the earth, and their words to the end of the world." As previously indicated, God gave me that Scripture in 1975 and it has been self-fulfilled in my ministry in the last number of years, though I have been slow to receive and to put into practice many of God's promises, but I am pressing on. Be strong (1 Kings 2:2) as David charged Solomon.

It is interesting to note that Genesis covers 50 chapters and covers a period of approximately 2,300 years. The story of creation is told in 800 words. Half of the book is about the development of Abraham's character, a third on the development of Joseph. God is no respecter of persons but He is a great respecter of character. If we do not want to be a floater, sailing down as driftwood on a stream, we are to stem the current that would drown us and stop us. Be a man. Don't go with every flow. Test it by the Word of God (Proverbs 22:21). Without a definite everlasting purpose in life, life would become a failure, which is the reason there are so many bones bleaching the highways of this world today. Those who once started well with bright shining faces, taking the platform every week, who never expected to go anywhere that God planned. You can be big physically but a pigmy in God's sight. You can be a grasshopper and conquer a giant. It does not depend on the size of your body but the quality of your soul. Don't be a 'penny-a-bunch' fellow. Show yourself a man, not a mighty midget. True manhood means self-control. We know that Samson was a giant in strength but a baby in self-control. Form good habits young, because a thread can be broken but a rope will hang you. Before getting into the hopper, take a look at the grit coming out of the other side. Have good friends, read good books. If you feed yourself on the Dandy and Beano, you will become a comic. A diet of dailies may deny your destiny but a diet on the Word of God will build you up.

Care for your own vineyard

Many occupations have a disease peculiar to their nature. The miner is subject to silicosis, creosote workers to dermatitis, painters to colitis, and so we could continue. The perils in the life of a man of God, a leader whose spiritual life and ministry has succumbed to the inroads of the disease of backsliding has no compensation. The worst disease is backsliding or not knowing that the Holy Spirit has departed from us. The peril of being absorbed in the externals of spiritual work, feeding, encouraging, counselling, warning and planning for others, can all cause neglect of your own soul, your own family and church. I believe that this is why we read in Song of Solomon 1:6: "They made me the keeper of the vineyards, but my own vineyard I have not kept." There were times in the early parts of my ministry when I was invited to conventions and other meetings and in some way I neglected my own church and family. However, when my children became teenagers, I had to apologise to them for not being around at times when I should have been. I truly thank God for Sylvia who has been a fantastic wife and mother, through tough and good times.

More important lessons:

Deal thoroughly with sin (Romans 7:24). It is so easy to preach against sin and still allow things, even small things in our own lives. We are to deal with them. If we are out of sorts with people in our own family it is best to put those things right in order to be effective in ministry. To 'never let the sun go down on your wrath' is good advice. Do not go to bed and be out of sorts with any of your family. Never own anything. This is a strange thing to say, but Acts 2:44-45 teaches us to never hold on to something so tightly that if you lost it, your life would collapse. We are passing through this life. We are on our way to heaven and we are to invest in the Kingdom of Heaven. I know what it is like to hold on to things and feel that you could not live without them, and then suddenly they are taken away, whatever they may be. Is there something right now that you feel that you cannot let anyone else touch, no one else could ever even borrow it? Never own anything. Hold lightly to the things of this world. This does not mean that God will not give you things, of course He will, but we are to be prepared to put them all on the altar of sacrifice. Never depend on anything to keep you going in the work of God, as God Himself will keep you.

Of course we have no real rights

We do not fight for the defence of ourselves (2 Tim. 2:24; 1 Sam. 17:47). When we came to Christ, we came under new ownership and new directorship. We are not to let people walk over us and wipe their dirty boots on us but, for Christ's sake, we are to walk humbly before Him and we are to walk fully dependent on Him. There are times when we want to fight our battles. But you could fight your own battle and lose or be very weak at the end of the day. Or you can put the battle before the Lord, as the battle is the Lord's. Never pass on anything about anyone that will hurt them. What a challenge that is (James 3:5, 6; 4:11). God expects good manners and etiquette from those who sit at His table. There are rules when we come around the table with other folk.

We are to respect people and to keep watch over our conversation. Never accept the glory, only encouragement (John 4:10). It is great to be encouraged and we need to be great encouragers, but once we accept any glory, we are on a downward track as all the glory belongs to the Lord. I believe that we are to watch our possessions, as they can be dangerous. In Matthew 6:33 it says: "Seek ye first the Kingdom of God, and His righteousness, and all these things shall be added unto you" (AV). Zeal without knowledge is dangerous. Paul of Tarsus had plenty of zeal but he persecuted and murdered the Christians. Knowledge without wisdom, having the ability to do so much but not the wisdom to do it in the right time and with the right attitude. It is very significant that knowledge and wisdom go together so much in Scripture. Our abilities can become our greatest handicaps. Your natural ability can puff you up and be a block to dependence on God. Ability without character is dangerous. God looks for character as a major attribute. Responsibility without faithfulness is dangerous. Consistency is needed in God's work today. Position without passion will never amount to much; I have come across so many men and women who are square pegs in round holes. Do not try and carve out a shape for yourself but let God move you on into something that He desires for you in which you will find greater fulfilment than in following your own will. And then, fulfil your calling. You cannot function without unction. The secret of a man is the fullness of a man. Whatever dominates a man's life, dominates him. You may be knocked down but not knocked out. Paul, who had so many tremendous experiences, says, "...having done all, to stand." I remember reading about David Brainerd, that wonderful missionary to the Indians, who said, "Do not think it enough to live at the rate of common Christians." Ezekiel 22:30 says: "So I sought for a man among them who would make a wall and stand in the gap before Me and on behalf of the land... but I found no one." People need the Lord. The greatest accomplishment is to see sinners come to Jesus. It has been the passion of my life.

One of the greatest lessons that one can learn today is that at the end of your life, as you look back, what really counts is what has been done for Jesus and what has lasted. Be careful of the roots of jealousy that bring a distorted picture of yourself. Do you know how really beautiful and valuable you are to Jesus? We live in a performance-orientated world. It presses us into its mould of conformity. God has made us unique and we are precious to Him. Jealousy is the universal motive of the human heart, in all work and skill development, unless the life of Jesus is being lived through us on a daily basis (Eccl. 4:4,6). Jealousy is totally ruthless and uncaring and there seems to be so much of it about today. It may be in a different guise. It is called 'competitiveness'. Here, like the salmon leaping up the waterfalls of opportunity, men struggle to dominate others and falsely believe that they will then amount to something. Poor, exhausted child. The Kingdom of Jesus is not like that at all. The basis of your value and your beauty is really your uniqueness. You are "fearfully and wonderfully made". Do not have an inflated picture of self-pride (James 3:14). Humility is to see ourselves as we really are and humble ourselves under the mighty hand of God.

Beware of a twisted picture of God in His justice, asking: 'Is God always fair?' Of course He is. So why are we bent out of shape when somebody else receives a blessing? We are failing to see the mercy of God in our own lives. This brings fear and insecurity in our relationship with God. Why do we become depressed when that other woman has a new baby or that other family moves into a beautiful new home? Why are spiritual leaders encouraged yet strangely discouraged when they hear reports of great success in another person's ministry? David said in Psalm 49:16: "Do not be afraid when one becomes rich, when the glory of his house is increased." Let us be content in the arms of Jesus.

Are you busier than ever in Christian service but accomplishing little and enjoying it less? Do you feel depleted and fatigued? Instead of being energetic, do you have physical ailments that won't go away? Burn-out is a constant threat to Christian leaders and indeed to all Christians these days. Christian believers are especially susceptible to burn-out. This is true for a number of reasons. We are particularly susceptible to burnout because of our typically idealistic perfectionist aspirations and high expectations. Paul says in Galatians 6:9: "Let us not be weary in well doing: for in due season we shall reap, if we faint not" (AV). Let us not slacken our exertions by reason of the weariness that comes from prolonged effort in habitually doing good. We shall reap if we do not become feeble through exhaustion and faint. Perhaps Elijah is the best illustration here. James reminds us that Elijah was a man of like feelings as ourselves and in fact common forms of burn-out may well be called the 'Elijah Syndrome'. We can learn from these men. Learn from the Scriptures. It is also important to recognise and reject false cures. People will come to us with all their problems, to find rest and to get away from those things that are burdensome. The burden of the Lord is easy. His yoke is easy. His burden is light. Sometimes the burning heart leads to an itching ear. The frantic search for new, titillating, religious experiences is on and some of them are not going to do us any good and may even do us harm. Prayer, meditation, rest and prioritising may just be of some help. Another cause of burn-out, especially in believers, is false motivation. The converse is service motivated solely by the love of Christ. "I will steadfastly refuse to gratify the devil by being discouraged," was a text that was on the mantelpiece in Kenley Bible School when I was there many years ago. Another said: "Let me ever love thyself more than thy service." I will never forget those wise words from Bible school days.

Another method of avoiding or curing burn-out is continual renewal, physical, emotional, mental and spiritual. We receive spiritual renewal by being filled with the Spirit and the Word of God (Eph. 5:18; Col. 3:16). Individually we must break out of those old stale patterns. 'Groove' and 'grave' are derived from the same word. I dare you to take an afternoon off to do something new. Find a new hobby, take up a new sport, read a new book. The psalmist's words seem to be directed at the problem of burn-out. "I had fainted," or "(think what trouble I would have been in) unless I had believed that I would see the goodness of the LORD in the land of the living" (Psalm 27:13). I was brought up being told that one should never take a day off a week. "You should always be on call for the Lord." This is partly right but it can result in breakdowns of health in later years. Distancing, detachment, withdrawal are allies of burn-out. So fellowship and closeness and mutual edification are foes of burn-out. Have good friends.

Recognising hurt

It is really not that complicated to recognise hurt, especially if bitterness has set in. Let's think of some of the characteristics of a hurt person. They show a lack of concern for others. A bitter person cares very little for anybody else. They are very sensitive and touchy. They become very possessive with just a few friends and rarely ever have any really close friends. They tend to avoid meeting new people. They show little or no gratitude at all, usually speaking words of empty flattery or harsh criticism. They hold grudges against people, often for a long time. They find it extremely difficult to forgive. They often have a stubborn or sulking attitude, usually unwilling to share or help anybody. They end up experiencing mood extremes, being very high and happy one minute, and then the next thing you know is that they are so low that they cannot reach up and touch bottom. The worst thing about bitterness and hurt is that it does not stop. It keeps getting worse. It may only start as a little seed but then it grows and festers into a very dangerous ulcer. Hebrews 12:15 says, "Looking carefully lest anyone fall short of the grace of God, lest any root of bitterness springing up cause trouble, and by this many become defiled." There is a question there. Does bitterness just hurt the person who is bitter? No, the Bible says that many people can be hurt by one person's bitterness. While we see the outward signs of hurt, we can also thank God, looking at the positive answers and helps that will cause us to overcome this particular mountain you may be facing now.

How to get out of the bitterness trap

Make a list of the people who have hurt you. This is pretty easy to do, and underneath each name write down everything that they have done to hurt you. Secondly, make another list of the things you have done to hurt them. That's the hard one, as we don't remember those things quite as easily. The point of making this list is that it is time that you saw your wrong. The key to forgiveness is to see how much you have done wrong. Then take a good look at how you have hurt the Lord. Once you have finished your list, you have still got the main job to take care of, get down on your knees and ask God to show you what you have done to hurt Him. God knows what it is like to be deeply hurt too. Genesis 6:6 says that: "The LORD was grieved that He had made man on the earth, and His heart was filled with pain" (NIV). That 'heart filled with pain' phrase literally means to have difficulty in breathing. God made this beautiful creation and then He sees people not only hating and killing each other but also hating Him. All that hurt goes deep into His heart. We forget that God has a perfect memory. We only see a little bit, but He sees it all continuously. We only live for a short time; He lives forever. When God looked at the world He had made he gasped with pain and horror; it hurt Him. Then pray and ask for the forgiveness of God unto man. It is not a complicated thing but it is costly. You need a slice of time on your own but you must do this first before you can help other people. Get out the list of how you have hurt God and others and let the Lord break you and then begin to put things right. Someone once said that it is a good thing to destroy the files in your mind. Remember the list of things that others have done to hurt you. Remember the filing cabinets in your mind. Take out all the files and get rid of them. Tear up your list and burn it. You must release it all to God. Forgiveness is opening the filing cabinet before God and clearing the debts. In Matthew 6:14 and 15 it says, "If you forgive men their trespasses, your heavenly Father will also forgive you. But if you do not forgive men their trespasses, neither will your Father forgive your trespasses." It is a choice you must make in response to God's offer of forgiveness to you. We can be dangerous men and women for God: those who are having an effect upon our neighbourhood, upon our towns, cities, churches and our nation. Stephen was a man full of faith and the Holy Ghost. Do you see the word 'full' recurring? Everyone is full of something. Some are full of themselves. Some are tired of certain people because they are always full of problems so that they themselves become the biggest problem. Some are full of plans and ambitions. Stephen was full too. He was full of the Holy Ghost, full of grace, truth, power and wisdom. Whatever fills a man, drives a man. The secret of a man is the fullness of a man. One of the greatest lessons that I have learned is that, unless we are full of God, we will have very little effect on people around us. The power of God's Spirit is not an optional extra. When God does anything big He does it through the Holy Spirit, whether creating the world, at the incarnation, putting the seed into the woman by the Holy Ghost, or at Calvary when He offered up Himself. He had power to lay down His life and to raise it again. When He went to heaven He sent the Holy Spirit. This is the greatest lesson to learn that when we are full of God, emptied of self, our old sinful nature not having the pre-eminence, we are more than conquerors through Him that loved us. You are a victor. You are a conqueror. Gideon did not think so either, when God said, "You mighty man of valour." He was a weakling but in God's strength you can overcome every mountain that is before you today. Have a good day mountain climbing.

CHAPTER THIRTEEN

Lessons learned for leaders

At a leper colony in India, at noon a gong sounded for the midday meal. People came from all parts of the compound to the dining hall. All at once peals of laughter filled the air. Two young men, one riding on the other's back, were pretending to be a horse and a rider. They were having loads of fun. As the visitor watched, he was told that the man who was carrying his friend was blind and that the man being carried was lame. The one who couldn't see used his feet and the one who couldn't walk used his eyes. Together they helped each other and they found great joy in doing it. Imagine a church like that. Each member using his or her strength to make up for the weakness of others. That is what should be happening in every congregation of believers. Paul likens spiritual gifts to various parts of the human body. Eyes see, ears hear, hands work, feet move the body forward, all are essential and when each fulfils its function, the whole body benefits. All of us have weaknesses but we also have strengths. We are all different but God has given each of us at least one gift to use for the good of the Church. We need one another. In Christ's body there are no nobodies. Paul says in 1 Corinthians 12:22, "Those members of the body which seem to be weaker are necessary." I guess that there are some hills to get over here. Hills of low self-worth, hills of inadequacy and feelings that God has passed us by. These are certainly hills that we can get over on our trip up the mountain.

Great leaders inspire us to go places we would not go on our own and to attempt things which we never knew we had in us. The privilege of leadership is a high calling and an adventure too. Conversely, I believe what Dr John Maxwell says is correct: "He that thinks he leads, and has no one following him, only takes a walk." There is a price to be paid, sometimes it is opposition from within and sometimes it is opposition from without.

Some say that it is God who provides the gifts and others say that people are 'born leaders'. No! Only men and women who know themselves and recognise who they are, and then have made themselves available to God to make them better than they were, are the answer. 'Born leaders' would mean that God had favourites. It depends on our surrender and availability. We can develop the gifts but it is futile to copy other people's gifts or to imitate them. A genuine leader must have the humility not to be threatened by those who are close to him. For God is raising you up for a specific purpose. If others seem to be getting on more than you, accept it humbly. Is training advisable? Yes, if the opportunity is given to you. The school or group of the prophets in 1 Sam. 19:20, the school or group at Bethel (2 Kings 2:3) and at Gilgal (2 Kings 4:38) are examples. These schools were the forerunners of the present day training centres and their purpose was to develop and educate in the function of leadership. Moses trained Joshua, Elijah trained Elisha, Jesus trained His disciples, Paul trained Silas and Barnabas, Timothy, John Mark and others. Anything will go stagnant unless people are trained for positions of authority. We shouldn't first of all look for natural ability but for the call of God on a person's life.

Not all pastors have great powers of leadership and not all leaders are good pastors. There comes a mingling of both. Leadership is dangerous because while decision-making people can move mountains, leaders in the wrong position can do irreparable harm. There may be greater natural ability than spiritual ability. The greater the position, the greater the opportunity to make wrong decisions but also the ability to make many more opportunities. Good leaders are scarce. What a fine Scripture we have in Ezekiel 22:30. Some of the greatest lessons that I have learned in my life can be taken directly from these Scriptures, and some of the greatest lessons that I have learned have come through my mistakes. Leadership is influence, simply because we are taking people where they have never been before. Leadership is lonely and yet accountable. Accountability is the safeguard. Dictators don't like it. Training leaders requires training of attitude and character building as well as inspiration and faith, for mountain climbing and rock breaking. As I have quoted previously: "He that thinks he leads and has no one following, is only taking a walk." Superiority of attitude is so dangerous. This is why Jesus manifested and expected that those He would lead would be a different kind of leader. Weep with those who weep, not with those who sulk. There is a danger of being carried along by the anointing of the uniformed ladies' choir when their final crescendo brought deafening applause but a distinct break in the flow of the anointing of God's Spirit was also experienced. So often it happens that, when the preacher gets up to preach, with his scraps of paper and scribbled notes, he has prepared his message, received between the football round up on Saturday night's television and the struggle to keep his tired eyes open, before he eventually succumbs to bed. Someone tells him that the Holy Ghost has left the service; but the organised programme might carry him through just one more time. After all, the programme took longer to prepare than his sermon! The predictability of the 40-minute sing-song must be changed. The Word of God must not be last on the pile of priorities. The importance of the Word of God must be discerned and never relegated to a minor place in the programme. There must be an all-embracing love for the people to whom we minister. Hans Finsell in his book says, "People will never care how much you know until they know how much you care." Are people an interruption? Not if we are listening. Leaders are called to be pioneers. To sit where people sit and not to consider them to be a troublesome interruption. We must know that there is no point in taking on Mount Everest if we have not climbed Mount Snowdon first. It is dangerous to have a man who is so expansive in his vision, taking us into huge expensive projects without supplying the ability to accomplish and to see the task through. Leadership is for the long-haul. God's man never quits half way and leaves others to finish off the job. While he is a dreamer, he is also an accomplisher.

I believe that Satan would have many sit behind a desk and become an administrative pastor, a professional preacher, a polished politician with all the answers, spending more time behind the desk doing mundane paperwork than studying the Word of God. This is not what it is all about. It is imperative that you get out where the people are, because there you get the heartache, the call, the burden and the fire to reach the lost. May God give us wider vision and the ability to encompass that great directive of Scripture: "By all means save some." If we lose the common touch, we lose what Jesus had in abundance. Do not isolate yourself from those you are called to win, but feel the heartbeat of the nation in which God has placed you to serve. However, we need to be careful to have a balance regarding these very important issues.

Paul put it in another way. He said, "I am a prisoner of Jesus Christ." When we become a prisoner of Jesus Christ we are then totally free. Sometimes travelling on a difficult and tortuous path, like Paul did, can do us good. When Paul recognised who the jailer was and that God had control over his life, he knew that his end was not yet and there was still much for him to do; he led the jailer to Christ.

Moses was a man of action but was once sidelined. If you are sidelined this does not mean that you are out of line with God. No one could do the job as well as Moses but he was sidelined. He lost his own strength and ability. Stripped to serve, he came out of the wilderness as the deliverer. I came out of Cheadle Royal Hospital, and the Priory in Altrincham a different man too. After 40 years of discipline, Moses came out and led a nation into submission, because the power of the King was behind him. Returning to service in Bolton was one of the great joys of my life. I remember some Australian brothers visiting the church, talking about vision and the extension of God's Kingdom and the largeness of churches in Australia and yet they said growth came because we 'set realistic goals'. I remember Enid Brooks leading me to the front for prayer and that these brothers prayed for me. That night God touched my life, I received a new freedom in preaching, a new fire in my soul. God does not put powerful weapons into the hands of children. We might choose a meat or milk diet, we make the choice – that is if we know the difference!

A well-known lecturer in college said there are four stages of leadership through which a leader passes with his congregation. In the first year, he is idolised; in the second, he is analysed; during the third, he is criticised and in the fourth, paralysed. I trust that our perception is higher than this. Prioritise on your personal relationship with the Lord Jesus Christ and there will be no reason that you cannot say, as I can by the grace of God, 50 years serving Jesus and I am not out yet! I am praying and believing for a move of God's Spirit, a revival move in Great Britain again. We have emphasised so much over the last number of years, the work of the ministry. In Ephesians 4:11,12, the Bible teaches us about the fivefold ministry gifts of Christ: apostles, prophets, evangelists, pastors and teachers. There is the danger that we talk about them and even pray for them but are afraid to acknowledge the men when God puts them in our way. Such men have been raised up for the perfecting of the saints, for the work of the ministry and for the edifying of the body of Christ. Someone called it 'the error of the misplaced comma'. We have come away from those days when we felt that the pastor had to do it all. He can't. We do sometimes have the ludicrous situation of more leaders than sheep in some fellowships. The brothers must not be upset because they are left out. However, when there are more leaders than sheep being led, the leaders go to war against each other! The pastor who has been brought up on a 'do it all' ministry for years and years will probably die young. The work of the minister, in Ephesians 4:11, is the work of the fivefold ministry gifts of Christ to the church. Let us recognise them. Delegation has been the saviour of many pastors. Learning to delegate will take trust. Quite often, wives are a tremendous 'help-meet' in this important ministry. Not a 'help-mate' but a 'help-meet'.

There is a big difference. A 'help-meet' stands alongside you. She is someone on an equal with you, to complement you in governing and keeping order in the house (Genesis 2:18). In a similar way it would seem logical that one minister could not do as well as two or more could do in governing God's family. In the beginning, the family unit was created. God established it by creating Adam and Eve. We might label them 'plural parents'. It is possible today for a single person to have a family. However, to have complete fulfilment you need a couple to have a complete family. It is God's design that a person should not try to have a family alone. God has ordained that a man has a wife and a woman has a husband so that, as a team, they function as a family unit. So it is reasonable that if God requires a team ministry in a family unit then, beyond all doubt, a team ministry in the House of God would be beneficial, especially in a growing church. We have a New Testament pattern here. It presents its problems, there are risks, there are dangers but the blessings are there for us to see and to understand. In the greeting of his letter to the Christians at Philippi, Paul addressed three groups of people: the saints, the bishops and the deacons. The saints are the gathering and congregation of all believers. The other two groups are the two offices in the church: bishops and the office of deacons. Deacons work, elders rule, they give rulership under Christ and we should be clear in our definition. It does not mean that because a deacon fulfils his ministry well that he steps up the ladder and therefore eventually becomes an elder. They are two distinct offices in the Church. Consider how a parental home is managed. In the parental aspect of a home there are two people: the mother and the father. They are not in competition, they simply have different roles. Similarly, elders and deacons are never to feel that they are in competition with each other. A wonderful example of team ministry is portrayed in Acts 13. There just happened to be five ministers there. Luke's mention of them shows that there was a recognition of their ministries. A team, not just of administrative staff, but the full complement of the fivefold ministry. May God help us to raise up patterns that follow the New Testament. It might be a dream, but a dream can come to fulfilment if we receive the directions from Almighty God. There is a leader amongst equals. Each council of elders has a president or chairman appointed. There must be one that carries the buck but does so with others helping him. The benefits are awesome. There is no doubt in the world that secular emphasis is taking away the responsibilities of mother and fatherhood, mixing them up and denigrating the family, but God has very clearly defined in Scripture the roles of man and woman. They are equal before God and equal in the home but with different roles. We must have checks and balances. In 1 Peter 5:2, 3 it says that the by-product of team ministry is much needed, which is seen in the very fact that Peter warned these elders not to abuse the eldership either by covetousness, or by begrudging and being jealous of others. What a value people on a team can be when they balance our fantasies with reality and check our unchecked opinions together. We need these men of God and, over the years, I have seen things change, some for the good and some for bad. If we are scriptural and biblical, God will keep us on the right lines. Probably the worst thing that was ever said to me was when it was felt that my ministry was irrelevant. Why irrelevant? Because I preached the Word of God and it was uncomfortable and maybe in contradistinction to the secular emphasis of the day. We must be prepared to meet confrontation with the grace of God.

If we keep our biblical vision in perspective we shall not be afraid to encourage diversity and variety. The strength of a team of elders is in its unique diversity and variety. Each is different. Each needs to examine its limitations, strengths and weaknesses. An elder must keep an eye out and oversee so that the right person is in the right place, doing the right job with the right gift.

Proper coordination makes for a smooth working team. Esteem one another as equals. The Lord said to Moses, "Take thee Joshua the son of Nun... and set him before Eleazar the priest, and before all the congregation; and give him a charge in their sight. And thou shalt put some of thine honour upon him, that all the congregation of the children of Israel may be obedient" (Numbers 27:18-20, AV). No one member is to aspire to dominate the team. The twelve apostles succumbed to this error in Luke 22:24 and Matthew 20:21. The early Church was plagued with the same tendency (3 John 9). Diotrephes loved to have the pre-eminence among the believers. No single elder is to strive for popularity over the others, neither is one to compete with another. This is why I suggest that each elder is not to develop a fleshly formed personality. This not only involves attitude but also involves conduct and dress. We should all dress modestly, not calling attention to ourselves by our appearance. Power corrupts the best of leaders. Absolute power corrupts absolutely (1 Corinthians 1:26-31). Take time to show appreciation to fellow labourers by a note, a gift, a word or an evening together. Encourage them privately and praise them publicly. Give credit where credit is due. Demonstrate pride in them. These are all lessons that I have learned over the past years. An elder can find fulfilment in ministry if he is not treated like a robot or a puppet. Allowing freedom to explore alternatives, to make mistakes, to ask questions like 'Is there a better way?', and guess what, he might just run across a better method, a cheaper process, a more positive, growing and exciting future. All are involved in this. One said, "Mind, money, morals, marriage, misgivings, ministerial roles." All have a part in the development of good leaders.

During his presidency, Abraham Lincoln was greatly respected and also greatly reviled. He plunged the nation into civil war. He was the president that people loved to hate. Those who opposed his views regarding the war on slavery as well as his efforts to keep the nation united were vocal and uninhibited in denouncing him. One day, during the darkest days of his presidency, Lincoln was walking down a street near the capital in Washington when an acquaintance caught up with him, and as they walked together the man brought up the subject of the growing anti-Lincoln sentiment flowing in Washington and throughout the country. With brutal honesty, the man related to Lincoln many of the stories outlining attacks on Lincoln and his policies. As the man spoke, Lincoln remained completely silent and absorbed in his own thoughts. Finally, the exasperated man asked, "Mr Lincoln, have you heard me? Are you listening to me?"

Lincoln stopped, looked directly at him and said, "Yes, I have heard you but let me tell you a story. You know that during the full moon it is the habit of all the dogs to come out at night and bark at the moon. This keeps on as long as the moon is clearly visible in the sky." Then he stopped speaking and continued his walk.

Confused by Lincoln's response, his exasperated companion persisted: "Mr Lincoln, you haven't finished your story. Tell me the rest of it."

Once again, Lincoln stopped and said, "There is nothing more to it; the moon keeps right on shining." President Lincoln was a good role model in managing criticism. Although he was aware of his shortcomings and knew that many highly respected and influential people disagreed with him, the president listened to criticism and still followed his own intuition, proving that his policies would eventually win over the critics and unify the country. One of life's challenging realities is that there are always people around us who are fault-finders: people who seldom see the good but are always quick to point out the negatives. All of us need to know how to deal with criticism, especially in the ministry. Don't be intimidated by criticism. The fear of criticism can affect you in many ways both trivial and serious. It can lead you to buy the latest fashions, and flashiest cars, because you fear being left behind by the times, and you may become out of step with everyone else. Refuse to be intimidated. Move from being emotionally fragile to emotionally resilient. Stick to your guns when you know it to be right. The antidote is to build emotional muscles so that you are stronger, more confident and less influenced by the opinions of other people. Be strong with the Lord's mighty power (Ephesians 6:10). Be strong and do not fear. "Take courage and work for I am with you" (Haggai 2:4). Look for wisdom in the criticism. While much criticism may come our way and be unwarranted, some criticism is not mere fault-finding but friendly advice. Eleanor Roosevelt once said, "Criticism makes very little dent upon me unless there is some real justification or something that should be done." Take comfort from the life of Christ!

Dale Carnegie wrote a book called 'How to Stop Worrying and Start Living'. He said, "Even if you and I are lied about, ridiculed, double-crossed, stabbed in the back and sold down the river by one out of every six of our most intimate friends, let's not indulge in an orgy of self-pity." Instead let us remind ourselves that that is precisely what happened to Jesus. One of his twelve most intimate friends turned traitor for a bribe that would be equivalent to four months wages in our modern money. Another one of his twelve most intimate friends openly deserted Him the moment he got into trouble, and declared three times that he did not even know Jesus, and swore as he said it. One out of six, that is what happened to Jesus. Why should you or I expect a better score? A lesson from the life of Christ is this: any time that we are providing leadership and engaged in making our home, our church, our neighbourhood a better place, there will be criticism. Be guided by wisdom from other leaders. Ronald Reagan once explained: "I don't pay much attention to critics. The world is divided into two kinds of people, those who can and those who criticise." Finally, when it comes to critics and criticism remember to follow the advice of Jesus: "Love your enemies, pray for those who persecute you" (Matthew 5:44). Praying for those who have hurt you brings an inner calm, a peace of mind, ultimately freedom from the pain of criticism, those who have hurt you most have probably been the most influential in your life to make you what you are today. The people who have said things about me, in front of my face and behind my back, are the ones that I can thank God for. Not immediately but after many years I have learned some excellent lessons. Living truth deals with inner deadness. "Sunday," said one preacher, "comes round with monotonous regularity." To hear him was to agree. He had achieved that for which science has been searching: light without heat. Brethren, we are called to handle the Word of Life, and the channels through which the life-giving Word is to flow must have partaken of that life. Ministerial backsliding is a danger. Whilst looking after other vineyards, you can neglect your own. The parable of pride, the sin of the sluggard, unconscious decay or the glory that faded, must be guarded against. "Forgetting those things which are behind... I press toward the goal for the prize of the upward call of God in Christ Jesus" (Philippians 3:13, 14). Sickness, financial reverse, friends that fail you, so many hills and difficulties but we are mountain climbers. We have had a go at Snowdon; we are now looking to Everest. The reformed pastor, Richard Baxter of Kidderminster, went through a time of despair. It was the despair of the indifferent response of the people that finally got to him. Utter godlessness, drunkenness, immorality, gambling and religious indifference were the order of the day, but the worst thing that he found was the indifference of his fellow ministers. He broke through the crust of godlessness, and he saw the district transformed by glorious revival. Many a pastor has become sour in his ministry like the soil around him. We are after all, all of us, temperamentally different. Our own mental processes must tackle problems, but we would do well to examine the ministry of men who have succeeded, to see what we can adopt from the fervency of their work for God, so that we can also learn from their lives. Your friends, your books, what you spend your time on, can all affect your character building. Do not crowd out the place of prayer. One of the great tragedies of our ministry is the readiness with which we permit ourselves to be crowded out. One writer said that the process of hindering prayer by crowding out is simple and goes by advancing stages. First prayer is hurried through unrest and agitation. Then time is shortened. Then it is crowded into a corner and depends on the fragments of time for its exercise. The place of neglected prayer must be avoided. I wonder if the continual singing of choruses at high speed, with the tempo of rock and roll, is not an attempt to create an emotional invasion which should be acquired rather from an overflow of blessing obtained in the private sanctuary.

There is a place for all kinds of approach. Prayer must

be exercised in order to avoid making the current transient traits and trends a substitute for Holy Ghost power. There are trads, rads and fads – traditionalists, radicals and those always swayed by the current flow. We urgently need balanced biblical and brave men to "rightly divide the truth of God" and expound the "whole counsel of God", and not a sickening amount of motivational drivel. A varied diet would lead to wholesome well-being and true growth of God's Church.

The spiritual decline of men of God is one of the saddest mysteries of our age. Men who were anointed to cast out devils have been overcome themselves by devils, like Judas. I think it is rare that leaders are guilty of the gross sins of the flesh, but nevertheless, whether great or small, we traditionalists must guard against every sin. Undoubtedly, when the sins of gluttony, drunkenness, gambling or others occur within the fellowship, they must be dealt with in a prompt and scriptural manner. The sins of leaders can be the more insidious sins of the spirit which rarely make an obvious appearance at the beginning. Being subservient to the people's declining prayer life, and idling time can lead to worse sins. Subservience to the people is a sin of the spirit. Guard your soul, guard your spirit, remember that there are those going about like wolves in sheep's clothing seeking whom they may devour. The sins and temptations of the flesh are so strong today. Watch the beginnings of anything that is going to devalue your soul and take your spiritual power away. Guard yourself with the Word of God, with wisdom and humility. If you refuse to face the real situation of your congregation you will fail, just as a leader who lives in a state of submission to the demands of a congregation is in fearful peril of ignoring the purposes of God. We must obey God rather than man!

In a couple of sentences, what are the biggest lessons that I have learned? What underlines all that I have written in this chapter? Leadership is not management, it is motivation. We are called to prepare God's people for works of service and to teach them to obey everything that Jesus has commanded.

Here are two excerpts from letters sent in response to our Radio Programme 'The Awakening Hour':

> From PO Box 39, Nathenje:
> *I want to thank you for your programme. All the messages by Pastor Terry have changed my life and my fellow primary school teachers. God bless Pastor Terry. Yours, Nelia Chaioula.*
>
> From Lauchenza, Mozambique:
> *This is my programme, I tape all the messages and teachings and teach them to my Bible study group. Pastor Terry Hanford is a man of God. I ask you how I can get his tapes for my friends in Mozambique. Yours faithfully, Lakison Chingipo.*

CHAPTER FOURTEEN

And there's more!

We have restarted Lifeline Ministries, which has laid dormant since the time we left Denton to this present time. I have talked about Lifeline Ministries in an earlier part of this book. The name has been resurrected and registered, and we now have the joy of coming under the banner of a company. My brother, Peter Yates, has a company called 'For Theophilus Ltd' whereby we have the benefit of gifts being designated and coming under the Gift Aid scheme and we have charity recognition. We have changed its image a little. We have a most interesting newsletter which comes out three or four times a year, which has been edited and despatched by Cyril Cartwright, but now by our most recent member on the charity, Paul Johns, who is our new Secretary. Anyone who wishes to receive further information please refer to our website: www.lifelineministries.co.uk. Or email: terryhanford@midforddrivefsnet.co.uk.

God allows you sometimes to go through great difficulties, maybe loss of a job, or marital problems, even to being in hospital for Him to reveal His purpose for your future. Keep yourself open to Him and, while there may be mountains which are greater to get over, the hills that you meet on your journey prepare you for the Everests you will yet overcome in His strength. Today I would say this: in sickness and in health, the Lord never fails. He can use you, He can shape your character and He can mature you. I know that God heals the sick today. Emphatically I know that it is

His strength and grace that keeps me and by His stripes we are healed.

And there's more! When you move into God's will in a specific new direction, Satan will try all ways to stop your progress. After relinquishing my eldership at 'The Bridge' Church my ministerial position ended on 31st December 2003. Sylvia and I sought God much for His direction for the latter years of our service for Jesus. There was no doubting that we were to reintroduce Lifeline Ministries, a ministry born of God in us in 1975. This is completely updated and we use the best equipment available. A team of dedicated workers has emerged. The devil has also been active. The chairman of our trust, Peter Yates, entered hospital to have his gall bladder removed, but serious complications meant him being in the intensive care unit in the Alexander Hospital for a month. For two weeks we had no verbal contact with him as he was kept sedated and was seriously ill. Now, thank God, he is home and back to his normal self under Margaret's watchful eye. I almost despaired as I saw the staff fight for his life. I sought for God's promise and found it: Psalm 118:17. The strain on my wife, Sylvia, is immense. I have often said no other woman could have seen me through the sickness times like my wonderful 'help-meet'. She too needs healing from her diabetes and deafness. No one receives a salary from Lifeline and all designated gifts go without deduction to the needs specified.

Ministry tapes and CDs are available by request. A list of books and CDs and a big selection of Scripture notes suitable for house groups or small study groups on various subjects is available. The harvest is plenteous, the labourers are few, by God's grace and as He permits I will face the future with my boots on and not carpet slippers. To Him be all the glory. I now have time to help smaller churches with ministry and advice if required, while remaining in membership at 'The Bridge' Church. I have a particular interest in the church at Horwich with its fine leaders, Phil and Alison Worsley, and also the pioneer work that Stephen and Joyce Mbwana are undertaking in Bolton. Wherever or whoever needs me I am ready to serve. Impossibilities are fuel to a dreamer!

Terry Hanford has spent 47 years in full-time ministry. Born in Aberaman, South Wales, he pastored and pioneered churches in the Assemblies of God in various parts of the UK. He has travelled the world preaching and teaching God's Word. He has been a broadcaster on several Christian radio stations and presently broadcasts to Central Africa from Trans World Radio.

This book is written with two things in mind. Firstly, that God can use the most insignificant person who is yielded to Him. Secondly, that in spite of ill health – for over 15 years Terry has been suffering with Parkinson's Disease – God still gives him strength to serve Him. As Terry often says, "I want to go to heaven with my boots on – not my carpet slippers!" People need the Lord and this motto drives Terry forward. He always thanks God for a wonderful wife, Sylvia, who cares for and supports Terry unstintingly.